First World War

and Army of Occupation

War Diary

France, Belgium and Germany

52 DIVISION
156 Infantry Brigade
Royal Scots (Lothian Regiment)
4th Battalion
1 April 1918 - 30 April 1919

WO95/2897/2

The Naval & Military Press Ltd
www.nmarchive.com
Published in association with The National Archives

Published by

The Naval & Military Press Ltd

Unit 10 Ridgewood Industrial Park,

Uckfield, East Sussex,

TN22 5QE England

Tel: +44 (0) 1825 749494

www.naval-military-press.com

www.nmarchive.com

This diary has been reprinted in facsimile from the original. Any imperfections are inevitably reproduced and the quality may fall short of modern type and cartographic standards.

Contents

Document type	Place/Title	Date From	Date To
Heading	WO95/2897-2		
Heading	52nd Division 156th Infy Bde 1-4th Bn Royal Scots Regt		
Heading	156th Brigade 52nd Division Disembarked Marseilles From Egypt 17.4.18 1/4th Battalion The Royal Scots Regiment April 1918.		
Heading	War Diary Of 1/4th Bn The Royal Scots (Q.E.R.) From 1st April 1918 To 30th April 1918 Vol XXXV		
War Diary	Surafend Camp	01/04/1918	03/04/1918
War Diary	Kantara	03/04/1918	04/04/1918
War Diary	Leasowe Castle	04/04/1918	11/04/1918
War Diary	On The Train	18/04/1918	18/04/1918
War Diary	Rue	20/04/1918	25/04/1918
War Diary	Rebecq	26/04/1918	30/04/1918
Heading	War Diary Of 1/4 Bn The Royal Scots (Q.E.R.) From 1st May 1918 To 31st May 1918 Vol XXXVI		
War Diary	Rebecq	01/05/1918	08/05/1918
War Diary	Mont St Eloy	08/05/1918	15/05/1918
War Diary	Hill Camp Neuville St Vaast	15/05/1918	15/05/1918
War Diary	Right Reserve 52 Div Sector	15/05/1918	18/05/1918
War Diary	Right Reserve 52 Div Sector Of Defence	19/05/1918	31/05/1918
Map	Map		
Miscellaneous	Strength Figures		
Heading	War Diary of 1/4 Bn. The Royal Scots (Q.E.R.) From 1st June 1918 To 30th June 1918 Vol XXXVII		
War Diary	Right Reserve 52nd Div Section Of Defence	01/06/1918	02/06/1918
War Diary	Reserve Billets St Eloy	02/06/1918	02/06/1918
War Diary	Left Section Of 52nd Div Section Of Defence Right Reserve	11/06/1918	30/06/1918
Operation(al) Order(s)	Operation Order No. 9 by Lieut Col A. Maclaine Mitchell D.S.O. Comdg 1/4th The Royal Scots	08/06/1918	08/06/1918
Miscellaneous	1/4 Bn. The Royal Scots (Q.E.R.) Administrative Orders	08/06/1918	08/06/1918
Map	Ref:- Maroeuil		
Miscellaneous	Ref Map Maroeuil 1/20,000 App 3		
Miscellaneous	Strength Figures	30/06/1918	30/06/1918
Heading	War Diary Of 1/4th Bn The Royal Scots (Q.E.R.) From 1st To 31st July 1918 Vol XXXVIII		
War Diary	Hills Camp Neville St Vaast	01/07/1918	14/07/1918
War Diary	Centre Sub Section Of Right Section 52nd Div Front	08/07/1918	14/07/1918
War Diary	Left Sub-Sections Of Right Section 52nd Div Section	15/07/1918	20/07/1918
War Diary	Lancaster Camp Mont St Eloy	22/07/1918	22/07/1918
War Diary	Mont St Eloy	23/07/1918	23/07/1918
War Diary	Bois d'Ochain	23/07/1918	29/07/1918
War Diary	Ecoivres	30/07/1918	31/07/1918
War Diary	Support Bn Hqrs B 27 C 70 10	31/07/1918	31/07/1918
Miscellaneous	Special Order Of The Day By Major General J. Hill C.B. D.S.O. Commanding 52nd (Lowland) Div	03/07/1918	03/07/1918
Operation(al) Order(s)	1/4th Bn The Royal Scots (Q.E.R.) Order No 13	06/07/1918	06/07/1918
Operation(al) Order(s)	1/4th Bn The Royal Scots (Q.E.R.) Order No. 17	29/07/1918	29/07/1918

Operation(al) Order(s)	1/4th Bn The Royal Scots (Q.E.R.) Order No. 18	28/07/1918	28/07/1918
Operation(al) Order(s)	1/4th Bn The Royal Scots (Q.E.R.) Order No 19	31/07/1918	31/07/1918
Map	Map		
Miscellaneous	1/4th Royal Scots (Q.E.R)	31/07/1918	31/07/1918
Map	Map		
Operation(al) Order(s)	Bn. Order No. 14	14/07/1918	14/07/1918
Miscellaneous	Administrative Order No. 14	14/07/1918	14/07/1918
Miscellaneous	Administrative Order No. 19	31/07/1918	31/07/1918
Heading	War Diary 1/4 Bn. The Royal Scots (Q.E.R) From Aug 1st To Aug 31st 1918 Volume XXXIX		
War Diary	Support Bn HQ. B 27 C 71	01/08/1918	21/08/1918
War Diary	Wanquentin	21/08/1918	28/08/1918
War Diary	Mercatel M 35.b 3.7	28/08/1918	31/08/1918
Miscellaneous	Warning Order	11/08/1918	11/08/1918
Miscellaneous	1/4th The Royal Scots (Q.E.R.) Amended Defence Scheme	06/08/1918	06/08/1918
Operation(al) Order(s)	1/4 Bn The Royal Scots (Q.E.R.) Order No 20 by Major J. Mowat Slater, Comdg.	12/08/1918	12/08/1918
Miscellaneous	Report On Operations	30/08/1918	30/08/1918
Miscellaneous	War Diary	31/08/1918	31/08/1918
Miscellaneous	Royal Scots Fusiliers Sept 1918		
Heading	War Diary 1/4th Bn Royal Scots Fusiliers 155th Infantry Brigade 52nd Division Vol V Sept 1918		
War Diary	Bullecourt	01/09/1918	02/09/1918
War Diary	Queant	02/09/1918	06/09/1918
War Diary	St Leger	07/09/1918	11/09/1918
War Diary	Nr. St Leger	12/09/1918	15/09/1918
War Diary	Moeuvres Sector	16/09/1918	17/09/1918
War Diary	The Field	17/09/1918	30/09/1918
Heading	War Diary For October 1918 Vol XLI 1/4 Bn Royal Scots (Q.E.R)		
War Diary	Ref Map Fame 57 C N E	01/10/1918	01/10/1918
War Diary	Canal Du Nord Beside Moeuvres	01/10/1918	07/10/1918
War Diary	Izel Lez Hameaux	07/10/1918	12/10/1918
War Diary	Ref Lens 1/100000	19/10/1918	19/10/1918
War Diary	Chateau De La Haie Ref Maps 1/40,000 Sheet W 4a 44. b.	20/10/1918	21/10/1918
War Diary	Auby	21/10/1918	29/10/1918
Miscellaneous	1/4 Bn The Royal Scots		
Operation(al) Order(s)	1/4th Bn. The Royal Scots (Q.E.R.) Bn Order No 28	01/10/1918	01/10/1918
Operation(al) Order(s)	1/4th Bn. The Royal Scots (Q.E.R.) Bn Order No. 31	19/10/1918	19/10/1918
Operation(al) Order(s)	Part Action Order No. 29	06/10/1918	06/10/1918
Operation(al) Order(s)	1/4 Bn The Royal Scots Bn Order No 30	07/10/1918	07/10/1918
Operation(al) Order(s)	1/4th Bn. The Royal Scots (Q.E.R.) Battalion Order No. 34	23/10/1918	23/10/1918
Operation(al) Order(s)	1/4th Bn. The Royal Scots (Q.E.R.) Battalion Order No 37	28/10/1918	28/10/1918
Heading	War Diary For November 1918 Vol XLII		
War Diary	Fresnoy (Ref Map 1/20000 France Sheet 44 NE	01/11/1918	09/11/1918
War Diary	Ref Map France 1/20000 Sheet 45 N W	09/11/1918	10/11/1918
War Diary	Herchies	10/11/1918	28/11/1918
War Diary	Montignies Lez Lens	28/11/1918	30/11/1918
Operation(al) Order(s)	1/4th Bn The Royal Scots Bn Order No. 41	10/11/1918	10/11/1918
Miscellaneous	War Diary	30/11/1918	30/11/1918
Heading	War Diary 156th Trench Mortar Battery 1st To 30th November 1918 Volume XVI		

War Diary	Battery Hqrs Mont Proy	01/11/1918	10/11/1918
War Diary	Herchies	11/11/1918	30/11/1918
War Diary	Thoricourt	30/11/1918	30/11/1918
Heading	War Diary Of 1/4th Bn The Royal Scots (Q.E.R.) From 1st 31st December 1918 (Vol XLIII)		
War Diary	Montignies Les Lens	00/12/1918	00/12/1918
Miscellaneous	Appendix 1	31/12/1918	31/12/1918
Heading	War Diary Of 1/4th Batt The Royal Scots (QER) For January 1919 Vol XLIV		
War Diary	Montignies Lez Lens	08/01/1919	18/01/1919
Miscellaneous	Attachment To War Diary		
Heading	War Diary Of 1/4th Bn The Royal Scots For February 1919 Vol XLV		
War Diary	Montignies Les Lens Belgium		
Miscellaneous	Appendix To War Diary	28/02/1919	28/02/1919
Heading	War Diary Of 1/4th Bn The Royal Scots (Q.E.R) For March 1919 Vol XLVI		
War Diary	Montignies Les Lens Belgium	01/03/1919	17/03/1919
War Diary	Soignies Belgium	17/03/1919	31/03/1919
Miscellaneous	Attachment To War Diary		
Heading	1/4th Bn The Royal Scots War Diary Volume XLVI April 1919		
War Diary	Soignies	01/04/1919	27/04/1919
War Diary	Dunkirk	28/04/1919	30/04/1919
Miscellaneous	Attachment To War Diary		

WO 95/2897(2)

52ND DIVISION
156TH INFY BDE

1-4TH BN ROYAL SCOTS REGT.

APR 1918-APR 1919

156th Brigade.

52nd Division.

9------------

Disembarked MARSEILLES from EGYPT 17.4.18

1/4th BATTALION

THE ROYAL SCOTS REGIMENT

APRIL 1918.

BEF ... 52

Vol 1

SECRET

CONFIDENTIAL.

WAR DIARY

OF

1/4TH BN. THE ROYAL SCOTS (Q.E.R.)

from 1ST APRIL 1918. to 30TH APRIL 1918

VOL. XXXV

15.8.31

Instructions regarding War Diaries and Intelligence Summaries are contained in F. S. Regs., Part II. and the Staff Manual respectively. Title Pages will be prepared in manuscript.

WAR DIARY
or
INTELLIGENCE SUMMARY
(Erase heading not required.)

Army Form C. 2118

1/4 R Scots (QER) April I

Place	Date	Hour	Summary of Events and Information	Remarks and references to Appendices
SURAFEND CAMP.	1-2nd		The Brigade Sports were carried out on 1st + 2nd April. Preparations were made for the move of the Battalion to KANTARA on the 3rd inst.	RBb.
KANTARA	3rd		The Battalion moved out from SURAFEND CAMP at 0515 and entrained at LUDD STATION at 0700 for KANTARA. On arrival, at about 2300, at KANTARA the Battalion marched to No1 Inf Base Depot where a hot meal was ready for all ranks.	RBb
LEASOWE CASTLE	4th - 5th		The Battalion was completed to 36 combatant officers and about 20 other ranks from hospital + courses of instruction rejoined. Clothing + ordnance stores were issued. The Battalion re-entrained at KANTARA WEST at 1900 and arrived GABBARY QUAY at 0540 on the morning of April 5th. embarking immediately on H.T. LEASOWE CASTLE. The 4th Battn The Royal Scots and the 4 Scottish Rifles and ASC. RAMC details, 156 Brigade Hqrs + Divisional General also embarked.	RBb.
	5th - 11th		The LEASOWE CASTLE remained in Alexandria Harbour. No leave ashore was granted to the men.	RBb

1875 Wt. W593/826 1,000,000 4/15 J.B.C. & A. A.D.S.S./Forms/C. 2118.

Army Form C. 2118

WAR DIARY
or
INTELLIGENCE SUMMARY

(Erase heading not required.)

Instructions regarding War Diaries and Intelligence Summaries are contained in F. S. Regs., Part II. and the Staff Manual respectively. Title Pages will be prepared in manuscript.

1/4 Battn The Royal Scots Q.E.R. April II

Place	Date	Hour	Summary of Events and Information	Remarks and references to Appendices
LEASOWE CASTLE	11th – 14th		The LEASOWE CASTLE sailed on 11th from Alexandria and was part of a large convoy of troopships escorted by destroyers. The voyage was calm and without incident. Very little training could be done owing to the crowded state of the ships. Gas drill, kit inspections and lectures were carried out. On the 14th at 2200 the Battalion disembarked at MARSEILLES and there entrained for NOYELLES leaving MARSEILLES at 0208.	ABC
ON THE TRAIN	18th – 20th		During the journey from MARSEILLES to NOYELLES, halts were arranged of about an hour or two hours at various stations and rations were issued and tea made. At 1600 after disentraining at NOYELLES the Battalion marched to RUE and camped in a standing camp in the grounds of the Chateau.	ABC
RUE.	20th – 24th		Whilst at RUE training was carried out for 4½ to 5 hours per day special attention being given to musketry, gas drill & route marching.	ABC
	25th		On the 25th inst the Battn entrained at RUE and leaving RUE at 1134 arrived at WIZERNES at 1830. On arrival the Battn marched to billets in QUELMES arriving about 2300.	ABC

1875 Wt. W593/826 1,000,000 4/15 J.B.C. & A. A.D.S.S./Forms/C. 2118.

Instructions regarding War Diaries and Intelligence Summaries are contained in F. S. Regs., Part II. and the Staff Manual respectively. Title Pages will be prepared in manuscript.

WAR DIARY
or
INTELLIGENCE SUMMARY

(Erase heading not required.)

Army Form C. 2118

4/ Battn The Royal Scots Q.R. April Page IV

Place	Date	Hour	Summary of Events and Information	Remarks and references to Appendices
Rebecq.	26th		At 0930 on 26 inst. the Battn left QUELMES and marched via WIZERNES to REBECQ arriving about 5.30pm in billets in the village.	Ref MAP BELGIUM 1/100,000 HAZEBROUCK Edition 2
			APB	
	24th–30th		Five hours training a day was carried out on 28th. 30th special attention being given to gas drill, bayonet fighting, and instruction of scouts, Lewis gunners and signallers. APB	
			General.	
			(1) The health of the Battalion throughout the month has been good. The change of climate has, so far, had no adverse effect on the health of the troops, in fact, a great improvement in smartness of movement and alertness has been noticed	APB
			(2) Reinforcement, strength, etc states are attached	
	30/4/18		A Bristowe Capt Lt a/Adj for Lt Col 4/ Bn. The Royal Scots Q.R.	

1875 Wt. W593/826 1,000,000 4/15 J.B.C. & A. A.D.S.S./Forms/C. 2118.

Additions to Strength

	O.	O.R.
From hospital	2	18
" Trade Tests	–	6
From U.K.	8	–
" Instructors' duty Zeitoun School	1	1
" Cadet Course, Zeitoun	1	–
	12	25

Deductions from Strength

	O.	O.R.
To hosp. (evac. out of Div. Area)	1	29
Left on duty with E.E.F.	1	10
" in Egypt for interview re Transfer to Royal Air F.	1	–
Left in Egypt for commission in Royal Air Force	–	1
Died	–	1
Transferred to R.E.	–	2
Capt. Hume-Gore to 8th Sea Rifles	1	–
	4	43

Candidates for commissions (from A.O.C. & A.S.C.) attached for instruction, rejoined units.

Strength of Battn.

	O.	O.R.
With Battn.	36	486
Detached within Div.	2	30
In hosp. in Div Area	–	11
	38	527

Attached – not included above

	O.	O.R.
Medical Officer	1	–
R.C. Chaplain	1	–
A.O.C. Sgt.	–	1
	2	1

Original

Vol 2

1625

CONFIDENTIAL

WAR DIARY

of

1/4 BN. THE ROYAL SCOTS (Q.E.R.)

FROM 1st MAY 1918 - - - - - - - - TO 31st MAY 1918.

VOL. XXXVI

Army Form C. 2118

WAR DIARY
or
INTELLIGENCE SUMMARY

Instructions regarding War Diaries and Intelligence Summaries are contained in F. S. Regs., Part II. and the Staff Manual respectively. Title Pages will be prepared in manuscript.

1/4 Battn The Royal Scots Q.E.R. (Erase heading not required.) May Page I.

Place	Date	Hour	Summary of Events and Information	Remarks and references to Appendices
REBECQ.	1st – 7th.		Training was carried out for five hours daily. The increased establishment of Lewis Guns from 16 to 36 per Battn necessitated the training of large numbers of Lewis Gunners. The attachment of an expert Bayonet Fighting and Physical Training Instructor to the unit and the training by him of two NCOs per Coy. made a great improvement in this branch of Battn training. On the 6th a demonstration was given by the REs in rapid wiring. Daily practice was carried out at the 30yds range and firing was done with and without gas masks ~~The~~ RPL both by riflemen and Lewis Gunners. On the 7th inst a Regimental Tactical Scheme was carried out in the neighbourhood of CLARQUES. The scheme had for its special object the training of subordinate commanders in taking independent action when faced by unexpected situations and also in report writing. Company training in gas drill, close order, platoon, and Coy drill, musketry, especially rapid loading and firing and control of fire was carried out also the training of runners, signallers and scouts under their respective officers. The weather except for occasional showers was good. On the 6th inst orders were received for the move of the Division to the MERICOURT SECTOR of the line to take over from the 4th Canadian Division and its transfer from the ~~XI~~ XI Corps to the XVIII Corps. This Battn RPL	Ref Map BELGIUM 1/100000 HAZEBROUCK Edition 2. RPL

Instructions regarding War Diaries and Intelligence Summaries are contained in F. S. Regs., Part II. and the Staff Manual respectively. Title Pages will be prepared in manuscript. 4 Battn The Royal Scots QER

WAR DIARY
or
INTELLIGENCE SUMMARY
(Erase heading not required.)

Army Form C. 2118

May Page II

Place	Date	Hour	Summary of Events and Information	Remarks and references to Appendices
			entraining at AIRE on the 8th inst. The mounted Personnel and transport preceding the unit by road on the 7th inst	RBG
MONT ST ELOY.	8th		At 1.30 pm on the 8th inst the Battalion less transport marched from REBECQ and arrived at AIRE at 4.15 pm where tea was made on an open space near the station. At 5.45 the Battalion entrained and left AIRE at 6.15 pm arriving at ACQ shortly after midnight. After detraining the Battalion marched to MONT ST ELOY and was housed in huts with wire mattress beds.	Ref. Map Belgium 1/100000 Hazebrouck Edition 2. Ref Map LENS 1/100000.
	9th – 15th		On the 9th inst the Training Programme was resumed on the same lines. Advantage was taken of the long and short ranges in the neighbourhood and all companies and the Lewis gunners carried out practices. All other ranks RBG of the Battn. bathed, no change of underclothing was available. The opening of home leave for the Battalion greatly improved the spirits of officers and men. On the 14th inst orders were received for the relief by the Battalion of 1/5 RSF in the Right Reserve of the Divisional front.	RBG
	15th.		On the 15th instant the Battalion embussed at MONT ST ELOY at 1 pm	

1875 Wt. W593/826 1,000,000 4/15 J.B.C. & A. A.D.S.S./Forms/C. 2118.

Instructions regarding War Diaries and Intelligence Summaries are contained in F. S. Regs., Part II. and the Staff Manual respectively. Title Pages will be prepared in manuscript.

Army Form C. 2118

WAR DIARY
or
INTELLIGENCE SUMMARY
(Erase heading not required.)

1/4 Battn The Royal Scots Q.E.R. May Page III

Place	Date	Hour	Summary of Events and Information	Remarks and references to Appendices
HILL CAMP NEUVILLE ST VAAST	15th		and was carried by motor lorry to NEUVILLE ST VAAST. At NEUVILLE ST VAAST Hqrs RB6 and two Coys (A + B) less 2 platoons took up quarters in HILL CAMP in corrugated iron huts. The remainder of the Battn was disposed as follows:–	Reference Map MAROEUIL 3.5.18
RIGHT RESERVE 52 Div Sector			D Coy: Garrison of Brown Line from TIRED ALLEY to WESTERN ROAD	
			C Coy: Living in Brown Line but at the disposal of O.C. 7 Scottish Rifles (holding firing line in Right Section) for the following purposes (a) half Coy to garrison TIRED ALLEY in event of an attack on the RIGHT FLANK (b) half Coy for counter attack as required.	See Rough Sketch appendix I RB6
			1 Platoon B Coy: Garrison SPUR POST.	
			1 " " " " FARBUS POST.	
			The relief was completed at midnight without casualty.	
	16th – 18th		On the 16th the 2 platoons of B Coy in HILL CAMP were moved to FARBUS POST and on 18th Battn Hqrs and A Coy moved to FARBUS POST. One platoon of B Coy moving to SPUR POST.	RB6
			WORK. A great deal of work on the trenches was required and all Coys in the line have been employed in improving the defences. Ration	

1875 Wt. W593/826 1,000,000 4/15 J.B.C. & A. A.D.S.S./Forms/C. 2118.

Instructions regarding War Diaries and Intelligence Summaries are contained in F. S. Regs., Part II. and the Staff Manual respectively. Title Pages will be prepared in manuscript.

Army Form C. 2118

WAR DIARY
or
INTELLIGENCE SUMMARY
(Erase heading not required.)

1/4 Battn The Royal Scots Q.R. May Page IV

Place	Date	Hour	Summary of Events and Information	Remarks and references to Appendices
RIGHT RESERVE 52 Div Section of Defence			carrying parties were supplied nightly to the 7 S R in the front line and also working parties.	ABb.
	19th 20 – 21st		The disposition of the Battn remained the same until 21st inst when a redisposition of C Coy (under the orders of 7th Scottish Rifles) was carried out. C Coy then being disposed as under:—	Ref map MARDEUIL 1/20,000 3.5.18
			1 Platoon, garrison TIRED ALLEY from CLYDE ALLEY to BROWN LINE	
			1 " " " " SUPPORT LINE to CLYDE ALLEY	
			1 " " Strong Point N.E. WILLERVAL (B.3.d.5.3 – B.3.d.6.4 – B.3.d.5.4 B.3.d.4.3	ABb
			1 Platoon in readiness for counter attack at B.3.d.8.8.	
			On the 16th + 18th two men were sent to hospital suffering from the effects of gas. The casualty on the 16th was caused by foul air in a deep dug-out that had been long disused the casualty on 18th was caused by a gas shell. On the 21st the enemy shelled FARBUS POST with 4.2 H.E. about 100 rounds being fired in three hours. One officer (2Lt W.C. BROWN) and 2 other ranks were killed by a direct hit on a dug out in FARBUS WOOD. Lt. L YOUNG was wounded.	ABb
			On the evening of 21st Battn H.Qrs and 1 Platoon of B Coy moved to THELUS CAVE – an enormous subterranean quarry.	

1875 Wt. W593/826 1,000,000 4/15 J.B.C. & A. A.D.S.S./Forms/C. 2118.

Instructions regarding War Diaries and Intelligence Summaries are contained in F. S. Regs., Part II. and the Staff Manual respectively. Title Pages will be prepared in manuscript.

WAR DIARY
or
INTELLIGENCE SUMMARY

(Erase heading not required.)

Army Form C. 2118

4/4 Battn The Royal Scots Q.R. — May — Page V

Place	Date	Hour	Summary of Events and Information	Remarks and references to Appendices
	22nd		Dispositions remained unchanged. Orders received to take over the RIGHT BATTN AREA of 52nd Division Section of Defence on 23 inst from 7 S. Rifles. Relief to be carried out by daylight.	ABb Ref Map MAROEUIL 1/20,000
			From the 15-22nd in addition to work on the defences and to carrying parties a considerable amount of training was carried out. 30 yd Rifle + Lewis Gun Ranges were improvised and men fired 5 rounds daily. Gas Drill was carried out and exercises in manning quickly battle positions from deep dug-outs were practised.	ABb 3.5.18
			The Battn experienced very little shelling from the enemy with the exception of that at FARBUS POST.	
			The weather during this period was warm	
RIGHT BATTN 52 Div Section of Defence	23rd to 31st		On the 23rd inst the Battn relieved the 7S.R in the RIGHT SUB-SECTION, each Battn taking over the dispositions of the relieving unit.	
			The defence of the right section of defence was as follows:— A.C.D. Coys (right to left) in Blue Line from Lived Alley to Western Road inclusive. The Blue Line was the main line of resistance and orders were received that it would be held to the last. The three Coys defending it provided 2 platoons in firing line and 2 in support and ready for immediate counter attacks.	ABb

Army Form C. 2118

Instructions regarding War Diaries and Intelligence Summaries are contained in F. S. Regs., Part II. and the Staff Manual respectively. Title Pages will be prepared in manuscript.

WAR DIARY
or
INTELLIGENCE SUMMARY

1/4 Battn The Royal Scots (Erase heading not required.) May Page VI

Place	Date	Hour	Summary of Events and Information	Remarks and references to Appendices
Right Battn 52 Div Section of Defence	Period 23rd to 31st		Behind the front system was the POST line defended by B Coy 4 R Scots and 3 sections + 2 platoons of 1/4 Scottish Rifles disposed as follows.	
			DURHAM POST — 1 Platoon B Coy	Ref map MAROEUIL 1/20000 3.5.18
			FOVANT POST — "	
			SUBURBS POST — "	
			BARNSLEY POST — "	
			VANCOUVER — 3 sections 1/4 SR	
			2 Platoons 4 SR near Battn Hqrs as mobile reserve to BLUE LINE.	
			Battn Hqrs B 9 b.0.5	
			The Posts were well dug + wired and each contained reserve SAA + rations.	AB6.
			In order to ensure co operation with the Bde on the right (51 Division) and to defend the right flank there were 5 mutual Bde Posts distributed down TIRED ALLEY from the WILLERVAL CHAUDIERE line to THELUS LINE.	
			(a) Junction of TIRED ALLEY with WILLERVAL CHAUDIERE LINE	
			(b) " " " " CLYDE ALLEY	
			(c) " " " " POST LINE	
			(d) " " " " BROWN LINE	
			(e) " " " " THELUS LINE.	

Army Form C. 2118

WAR DIARY
or
INTELLIGENCE SUMMARY

Instructions regarding War Diaries and Intelligence Summaries are contained in F. S. Regs., Part II. and the Staff Manual respectively. Title Pages will be prepared in manuscript.

1/7 Bn The Royal Scots QER (*Erase heading not required.*) May Page VII

Place	Date	Hour	Summary of Events and Information	Remarks and references to Appendices
	Period 23rd–31st		(b) & (d) being under Right Sub Section Commander (4 R Scots). 1 Rifle section + 1 Lewis gun section in each post. ½ supplied by 7SR and ½ by Battn of 51 Div. on right. Each supplying L.G. section to the posts supplied by them.	
			Artillery. Through liaison officer at Bn Hqrs.	
			3 Batteries 18 pdrs.	
			1 " 4.5 Hows.	
			M.Gs. 2 guns HUDSON TRENCH T28.c.05.80	
			2 " E of WILLERVAL B4c 15.80	
			2 " W of DURHAM POST B9 b1.0.25	
			2 " W of JUNCTION of TIRED ALLEY and RAILWAY near BROWN LINE	
			H.T.M.B. 2 " W of WILLERVAL	
			1 " S of MERSEY ALLEY near junction of alley with railway	RKf
			L.T.M.B. 5 " in BLUE LINE.	
			Communications. Telephone + Fullerphone.	
			Visual	
			Power Buzzer	
			Runners (relay)	
			Pigeons	
			S.O.S rockets.	
			Cyclist orderly to Bde.	
			Rations. Rations were brought up by light railway to LONGWOOD DUMP until 28 inst and from there carried to Coys by parties supplied by 1/7 SR. Afterwards pack ponies brought up Rations	

1875 Wt. W593/826 1,000,000 4/15 J.B.C. & A. A.D.S.S./Forms/C. 2118.

Army Form C. 2118

Instructions regarding War Diaries and Intelligence Summaries are contained in F. S. Regs., Part II. and the Staff Manual respectively. Title Pages will be prepared in manuscript.

WAR DIARY
or
INTELLIGENCE SUMMARY

1/4 Battn The Royal Scots 9 BR *(Erase heading not required.)*

Page VIII

Place	Date	Hour	Summary of Events and Information	Remarks and references to Appendices
	Period 23rd - 31st		along WILLERVAL ARLEUX ROAD to its junction with BROWN LINE at B4 c.6.7 and thence manhandled as before.	
			Water carried up by carrying parties from 7 SR from tanks near junction of Tired alley and Brown Line	
			Patrols. From the 24 inst 2 patrols of 1 officer + one or two sections were sent out nightly from our line to investigate enemy wire, to investigate suspected MG positions and to attack any enemy patrol encountered and if possible secure identifications. These patrols did not encounter any enemy. On several occasions our patrols were observed by the enemy from his line and were fired on by machine guns.	
			On the 29 inst 2Lt Hoy of this Battn was seriously wounded by MG fire, while in charge of a party covering a raiding party of the 1/7 SR. The raiding party were held up by MG fire and did not reach their objective.	ABG
			Artillery. There was considerable shelling of our line by the enemy by night throughout the period and enemy trench mortars caused considerable damage to the trenches. There was little sniping or machine gun fire directed on our line. By day, enemy shelling was intermittent and never heavy. It was directed chiefly against TIRED ALLEY. There was no sniping or machine gun fire by day.	

1875 Wt. W593/826 1,000,000 4/15 J.B.C. & A. A.D.S.S./Forms/C. 2118.

Army Form C. 2118

WAR DIARY
or
INTELLIGENCE SUMMARY
(Erase heading not required.)

Instructions regarding War Diaries and Intelligence Summaries are contained in F. S. Regs., Part II. and the Staff Manual respectively. Title Pages will be prepared in manuscript.

1/4 Battn The Royal Scots Q.R.

Page IX

Place	Date	Hour	Summary of Events and Information	Remarks and references to Appendices
	23rd	31st.	Works. Throughout the period much work was done on the defences. The damage caused by enemy shell fire on our trenches and communications was repaired. Duck boards re laid and barbed wire improved. The gas defences were thoroughly overhauled – new curtains fitted, gas alarms and battle station alarms ~~for~~ installed in deep dug-outs, Strombos horns were installed. The sanitary condition of the trenches was improved, trench stores of bombs, + S.A.A. were inspected and cleaned.	PBL
			Training. Daily training was carried out. Each man fired 5 rounds daily and instruction was given in the trenches on fire direction + control, judging distance. Frequent practice alarms were given to teach men to man their battle stations quickly. Schemes for immediate counter attack were explained to the men and the action to be taken by each post in event of the enemy breaking through on either flank was thoroughly examined and all ranks made conversant with the plan. S.O.S. tests by grenade + telephone were carried out with the artillery.	
			Leave. During the period 23 – 31 leave for other ranks has been	

1875 Wt. W593/826 1,000,000 4/15 J.B.C. & A. A.D.S.S./Forms/C. 2118.

Army Form C. 2118

WAR DIARY
or
INTELLIGENCE SUMMARY

Instructions regarding War Diaries and Intelligence Summaries are contained in F. S. Regs., Part II. and the Staff Manual respectively. Title Pages will be prepared in manuscript.

4 Battn The R Scots Q.E.R. (*Erase heading not required.*) Page X.

Place	Date	Hour	Summary of Events and Information	Remarks and references to Appendices
	Period 23rd - 31st		granted most sparingly owing to the necessity of keeping sections up to 4 other ranks in strength.	
		31st	On the 31st orders were received for the relief of the Battn by the 5 H.L.I.	
General.			Honours. The following awards were officially announced during the month for work during the advance in Palestine.	
			Lt Col A Maclaine Mitchell Bar to D.S.O.	A/36
			275194 CSM Grieve A.S. M.C.	
			250784 Pte Young W D.C.M.	
			Commissions. One NCO per week (not below full Cpl.) has been interviewed by the BGC since ~~to~~ 23 inst with a view to being admitted to a Cadet unit.	
			Weather. The weather throughout the month has been warm with very few wet days.	
			Reinforcements. Strengths etc are attached.	
			P Bristowe Capt Lt a/adj for Lt Col Comdg 4 Bn The Royal Scots Q.E.R.	

1875 Wt. W593/826 1,000,000 4/15 J.B.C. & A. A.D.S.S./Forms/C. 2118.

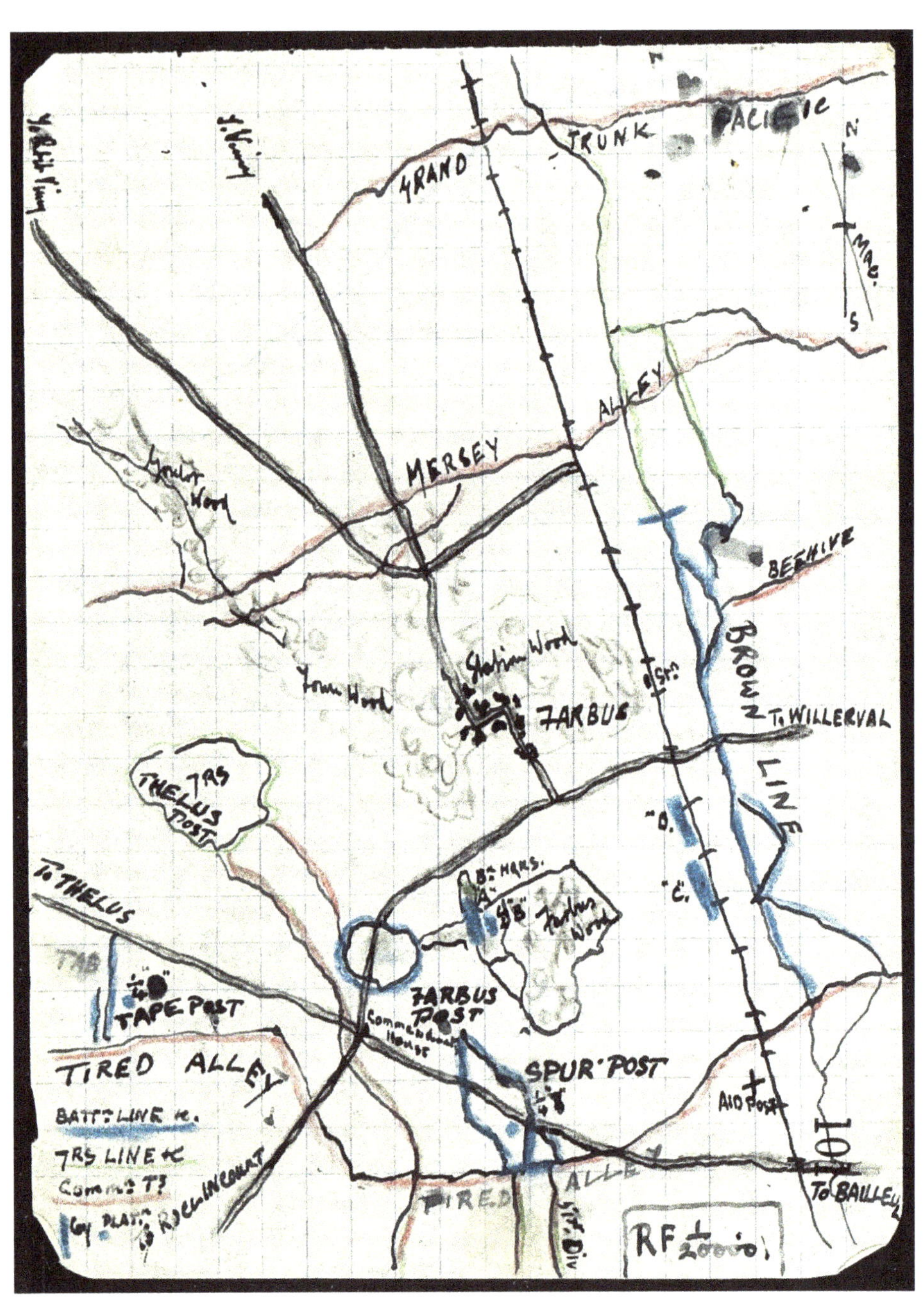

GRAND
TRUNK
PACIFIC
N
MAG.
S
MERSEY
ALLEY
Goulot Wood
BEEHIVE
BROWN
LINE
Station Wood
Town Wood
FARBUS
T. WILLERVAL
HQRS
THELUS POST
"D."
"C."
Farbus Wood
To THELUS
TAPE POST
FARBUS POST
Communication House
TIRED ALLEY
SPUR' POST
AID POST
BATT. LINE
HQRS LINE
To ROCLINCOURT
TIRED ALLEY
TO BAILLEUL
Div.
RF $\frac{1}{20000}$

WAR DIARY
MAY 1918.

Strength Figures

Additions to Strength	O.	O.R.	Deductions from Strength	O.	O.R.
From hospital	–	14	To hospital	2	94
" U.K.	1	57	Killed in action	1	2
" Egypt.	1	57	Wounded " "	2	5
" M.G. Co.	–	6	" Gas	–	4
" Leave to U.K.	1	–	To U.K. for Commissions	–	2
" Bde T.M. Bty.	1	–		5	107
Officers from 15th & 16th R.S.	3	–			
	7	134			

Strength of Bn. 1.6.1918.

	O.	O.R.
With Bn. (Including Q.M. Stores & Transpt.)	25	707
Nucleus personnel, Reinfn	5	13
Relay Runners' Posts	–	9
Bde. Signal Post	–	7
" Pioneer Co.	–	24
Courses of Instrn.	3	19
Leave to U.K.	6	19
Party to Base Depot for Med. re-classfn	–	9
Hospital (O.R. 7 days & under)	2	15
Sundries detached	1	36
	42	858

Attached:—
M.O. R.C. Chaplain
& A.C.C. S/Sgt.

CONFIDENTIAL

Vol 3

WAR DIARY

of

1/4 Bn. THE ROYAL SCOTS (Q.E.R.)

FROM 1st JUNE 1918 TO 30th JUNE, 1918.

VOL. XXXVII

1785

Army Form C. 2118.

Instructions regarding War Diaries and Intelligence Summaries are contained in F. S. Regs., Part II. and the Staff Manual respectively. Title pages will be prepared in manuscript.

WAR DIARY
or
INTELLIGENCE SUMMARY.
(Erase heading not required.)

1/4th Bn The Royal Scots (Q.R.R.) June 1918 Page 1.

Place	Date	Hour	Summary of Events and Information Ref Map Marœuil 1/20,000	Remarks and references to Appendices
Right Reserve 52nd Div' Section of Defence	1st	2nd Jun	Bde Artillery Group at the request of Battalion concentrated all its fire on machine guns & T Mortar emplacements & occupied posts in trenches in B5.	TDW
Reserve Billets St ELOY	2nd	10th	Bn relieved in line by 5th H.L.I. Relief completed without casualty. Bn arrived in Rest Billets at LANCASTER Camp at 8 pm. The 3rd inst was spent in bathing & reorganisation generally. From 4th to 10th five hours training was done per day, consisting of all specialist work, physical training, bayonet fighting, gas drill, musketry, firing Rifle Lewis Guns, close order drill & working out of small tactical schemes. An interesting forenoon was spent in a demonstration of Infantry working in cooperation with Tanks. Lectures were given to Officers on "Infantry Cooperation with Tanks & some recent gas operations". Every evening for the benefit of the men football matches were played & concerts & cinema performances given. Considerable discomfort was caused by the Billeting area being shelled intermittently by two long range guns but only two casualties occurred. It necessitated however a great deal of work in protective measures. The Battalion left the Billeting area by motor lorries to take up position in Right Reserve Left Section (O.O.) app1, taking over area from the 5th R.S.F. comprising VIMY-NOVA SCOTIA area as per sketch map attached (app 2). The relief was carried out smartly & without casualty.	TDW App 1. App 2 TDW

D. D. & L., London, E.C. (A8004) Wt W1771/M2031 750,000 5/17 Sch. 52 Forms/C2118/14

Army Form C. 2118.

Instructions regarding War Diaries and Intelligence Summaries are contained in F. S. Regs., Part II. and the Staff Manual respectively. Title pages will be prepared in manuscript.

WAR DIARY
or
INTELLIGENCE SUMMARY.
(Erase heading not required.)

1/4th Bn The Royal Scots (Q.R.) June 1918 (Page 2.)

Place	Date	Hour	Summary of Events and Information — Ref Map MAROEUIL 1/20,000	Remarks and references to Appendices
LEFT SECTION of 52nd DIV. Section of Defence Right RESERVE.	11-6-18 to 19-6-18.		The Bn immediately set to work on the defence of there line. Principal attention being given to wiring & blocks in Trenches, making of Elephant shelters for accomodation of garrison, Lewis Gun positions. On right of our line that occupied by A Coy (see sketch map) was subjected to occasional heavy shelling owing to the close proximity of our batteries, little damage however was done. Two platoons were used nightly for work with the R.E. signals, burying cable & one Company for removing dumps at 8th S.R. lines.	
	20-6-18		The Bn relieved the 7th Scottish Rifles in the Front Line. Three Coys being in the Firing Line (B.C. & D Coy) with A Coy in Reserve. Bn H.Q. were situated in the Tunnel in MONT FORET Quarries. The 7th Sco. Rifles sent out a patrol at night	
	21-6-18. & 22-6-18		Nothing of interest happened on these two days. Defensive patrols were sent out	
	23-6-18		A considerable amount of hostile shelling took place round Bn H.qrs, but no damage was done. At night a patrol under 2/Lt. dePhilip went out for the purpose of lying in wait for any Germans who might come out to repair their wire at T11 a.85.30, gaps having been cut in the early evening by the artillery. The patrol proceeded about 300 yds from our own wire when two parties of the enemy were seen. The patrol immediately took up a defensive position, but the enemy passed & unfortunately our patrol lost touch with them.	
	24-6-18.		A defensive patrol was sent out, it being relieved at 12.30 am by another but no enemy were seen.	

D. D. & L., London, E.C. (A8004) Wt W1771/M2031 750,000 5/17 Sch. 52 Forms/C2118/14

Instructions regarding War Diaries and Intelligence Summaries are contained in F. S. Regs., Part II. and the Staff Manual respectively. Title pages will be prepared in manuscript.

WAR DIARY
or
INTELLIGENCE SUMMARY.
(Erase heading not required.)

Page 3.

Army Form C. 2118.

1/4th Bn The Royal Scots. June 1918

Place	Date	Hour	Summary of Events and Information	Remarks and references to Appendices
[illegible]	25/6/18	-	The 20th Division on our left carried out a gas attack on enemy lines & owing to a change in direction of wind at 10pm the usual patrols were not sent out.	TSW TSW
	26th 27th		Defensive patrols ordered by the 52nd Division were carried out, but nothing of interest happened.	TSW
	28th	-	A redistribution of the Battalion took place today as per App. 3 attached.	
	29th	"	The Bn was relieved by the 1/7th H.L.I. & after relief proceeded to HILLS Camp.	TSW
	30th		The day was devoted to cleaning & rest.	
			General	
			Nothing of special interest happened during the month.	
			Two new drafts arrived for the Bn. 5 Officers joined viz 2/Lts W.R. LOCHHEAD W.A. HILLIARD, F.C. WIGHT, W.L. LISTON, A.W. DICKSON. 60 O. Ranks from the U.K. & 37 O. Ranks from the Base (from other Royal Scots Bns.)	
			The health of the Battalion for a week caused a little anxiety, but was soon taken in hand, an epidemic of influenza [illegible]	
			Intimation received that Capt. D.M. Stewart had been invalided home from Egypt wounded. Lieut J.C. Stewart invalided to U.K. on 4-6-18 sick. Lieut. L. Young invalided to U.K. wounded & severe debility	TSW
			The Bn deeply regretted the death from wounds of 2/Lieut A.B. Hoy	TSW
			The usual monthly Return is attached. (App. 4.)	
			Leave on a moderate scale has continued for all ranks.	TSW

D. D. & L., London, E.C. (A8004) Wt W1771/M2031 750,000 5/17 Sch. 52 Forms/C2118/14

Page 4

Army Form C. 2118.

Instructions regarding War Diaries and Intelligence Summaries are contained in F. S. Regs., Part II. and the Staff Manual respectively. Title pages will be prepared in manuscript.

WAR DIARY
or
INTELLIGENCE SUMMARY.
(Erase heading not required.)

1/4th Bn The Royal Scots — June 1918

Place	Date	Hour	Summary of Events and Information	Remarks and references to Appendices
			Two American N C Os were attached to the Battalion when in the Firing Line. On the 26th Lieut Bassett of the Corps Intelligence staff of the American Army joined us & stayed until the conclusion of our tour of duty in the Line. He showed great keenness & aptitude & made us proud that our Allies were determined to see it through	TDW

T. Drummond Wilson
Capt & Adjt
1/4th Bn The Royal Scots

D. D. & L., London, E.C.
(A8co4) Wt W1771/M2031 750,000 5/17 Sch. 52 Forms/C2118/14

Secret

Operation Order No 9. App I Copy No 2 ~~54~~

by Lieut Col A. Maclaine Mitchell DSO cmdg. 1/4th The Royal Scots

Ref Map. MAROEUIL 1/20,000

8th June 1918

(1). 156th Inf Bde will relieve 155th Inf Bde in the Left Section on June 11th & 12th

(2.) June 11th
7th Sco. Rifles relieve 5th K.O.S.B in Front Line Right Subsection
8th " " " 4th K.O.S.B " " " Left Subsection
4th Royal Scots " 5th R.S.F. in Right Reserve
7th " " " 4th R.S.F in Left Reserve.

A.B.C. & D. Coys 4th Royal Scots will relieve the corresponding Coys of the 5th R.S.F. thus: 'A' Coy BROWN LINE 'B' Coy KURTON TRENCH 'C' Coy at CANADA TRENCH 'D' Coy in VIMY.

June 12th / 156th L.T.M Battery relieve 155th L.T.M. Battery

(3) 4th Royal Scots will move by Motor Lorries to Barrier at LA FOLLIE FARM Road at S 28 d 8.8. starting about 12-15.

(4.) Guides will meet 4th Royal Scots at BARRIER S28.d.8.8. at 12.30 pm. These are being arranged for by the 155th Inf Bde 4th Royal Scots going into Right Subsection will move by HUMBER, ~~[illegible]~~ Trench

(5.) Movement will be by Platoons at 200 yds distance.

(6.) 7th Sco Rifles will detail an Officer to act as Debussing Officer at S28 d.8.8. & all instructions given by him will be carried out

(7) Advance parties consisting of one Officer per Coy. one NCO per Platoon. No 1 of all Lewis Guns in action Gas NCOs & a proportion of Signallers & Runners will go into the line on June 10th. Guides to take them to Bn H.Q. will meet them at Barrier S.28 d 8.8. at 3. pm.

(8) Communications, Trench Maps, Maps of Ho Maris Land, Defence Schemes, Log Books & Trench Stores will be taken over by Coys. The Bn. Sig. O. will take over Bn Hqrs.

(9.) Every Section will go into the Line 1 NCO & 6 men.
Every Company unable to carry out this order will report to Bn Hqrs immediately stating numbers deficient.
The following personnel in addition to the surplus to the above will proceed to VILLERS CAMP moving off at 1.30pm.
Major D.M. Slater ~~[illegible]~~ 2/Lt. Arw Philp.
A Coy Lieut H.W. Winchester M.C. 2/Lt J.B. Smart
"B" Capt James Gray M.C. D Coy Capt W.S. Ferrier.
C.S.M. Hughes B. Coy.
The following personnel will proceed to DALYS Camp:
Transport Officer & Transport
Asst Adjutant & Hqrs Adm. Personnel
Q.M. & Staff CoQ.M.S.'s & storemen.

10. Completion of Relief will be reported by Code Word "MERCY"

11. Brigade Hqrs at S 27 central
Battalion Hqrs at T.25 b.50.95 on NEW BRUNSWICK Road

12. Acknowledge

T. Drummond Wilson
Capt & Adjt
14th Bn The Royal Scots

Issued at 8.15pm

War Diary. 73

App. I

1/4. BN. THE ROYAL SCOTS (Q.E.R)

Administrative Orders
by
Lieut-Colonel A. Maclaine Mitchell D.S.O. Comdg.

Ref MAP MAROEUIL '20,000'

8 June 1918.

1. BILLETS

(a) All Billets & Camps must be left scrupulously clean, and a certificate signed by an officer of the incoming unit stating that the Camps have been taken over in a clean and sanitary condition will be forwarded to Bn. HQ immediately prior to moving out of present area.

(b) A list of Area Stores as per schedule to be handed over to incoming unit, will be forwarded to Bn. HQ. by 6 pm on 9-6-18.

(c) Certificates will be obtained from the Area Commandant that there are no outstanding claims for damage to Govt. property.

2. TRANSPORT.

The lines at present occupied will be vacated by 2 pm on 11-6-18 & certificates obtained that the lines were taken over in a clean and sanitary condition.

Transport will be brigaded at DALY CAMP (F.11.b.2.0.)

3. MOBILE STORES.

Mobile Stores, blankets & spare kits will be taken to DALY CAMP.

4 TRENCH STORES.

List of Trench Stores taken over will be furnished, as per Schedule, to reach Bn. HQ. not later than 24 hours after relief.

5 SUPPLIES

(a) Commencing 11th inst. supplies will be drawn from Refilling point at LEADLEY SIDING (A.2.c.6.8) + delivered to Transport Camp by the Supply Section of the Train.

(b) Rations will be taken to ZIVY Station + loaded on trains by 8.15 pm. daily for the following points:

Right Reserve Bn. - A + D Coy. + Bn. HQ.

BRUNSWICK DUMP (T.6.a.8.9.)

C + B. at CANADA DUMP (T.20.b.6.3.)

c) Coy. Q.M.S.^s will proceed each night with the rations from ZIVY + are responsible that the rations are delivered to their Coys.

d The QM. or T.O. will travel nightly with the Ration Train + report to Bn. HQ. for orders. The QM. will visit the Bn. when in the line at least every two days.

6 COOKING

Cooking by this Bn. may be done forward provided all due precautions are taken.

Fresh meat will be cooked at Transport Camp, forwarded by Light Rly. + heated up by the Sager Stoves.

7. RESERVE RATIONS. Distributed as follows:-

(a) Brigade Reserve.

		BISCUIT	MEAT
Right Res. Bn. (T.8.d.5.7.)		750	156

(b) Localities.

Right Res. Bn.	NOVA SCOTIA (T.21.a.3.3.)	600	576

8. WATER PICQUET.

The following picquet will relieve that found by 155. Inf Bde. at 2 pm. on 11-5-18.

Right Res. Bn. - 1 N.C.O. & 4 men for GOODMAN MAIN and VIMY (T.20.c.3.1.) "B" Coy. will furnish this.

9. AMMUNITION SUPPLY.

1. The ammunition is distributed as follows:
(a) With Companies
(b) Battalion Dump
(c) Forward Bde. Dumps
(d) Main Brigade Dump

2. Coys. restock from a convenient forward Brigade Dump on application to Bn. HQ

10. STRAGGLERS POSTS.

Stragglers Posts are as follows

S.11.d.4.2. S.18.c.9.5. S.24.b.4.6. T.19.c.2.5.

manned by personnel found by A.P.M.

11. PRISONERS of WAR.

Prisoners of War Cage. AUX RIETZ (A.8.c.5.7.)

12. SALVAGE.

Salvage Dumps are situated as follows:-

Right Line Bn. - CANADA DUMP.

Right Res. Bn. - BRUNSWICK DUMP.

13. MEDICAL.

Main Dressing Station. AUX RIETZ (A.8.C.5.0.)

Advanced " LA CHAUDIERE (S.18.C.9.5.)

Regimental Aid Posts.

Right Line Bn. T.6.c.6.0.

Right Res. " Battn. HQ.

14. BURIAL.

The following cemetries will be used:-

THELUS A.5.C.8.5. AUX RIETZ A.8.C.5.0.

An advanced collecting post is established at T.19.b.8.4.

Coys are responsible for taking bodies to the Station.

Coys will wire Bn. HQ when any bodies have been collected.

15. Acknowledge.

Issued at 8.15 pm.

T. Drummond Shiels

CAPT. & ADJT.

1/4th. B. The Royal Scots (Q.E.R.)

App 2

App. 2
War Diary. June '18

REF:- MAROEUIL 1/20000.

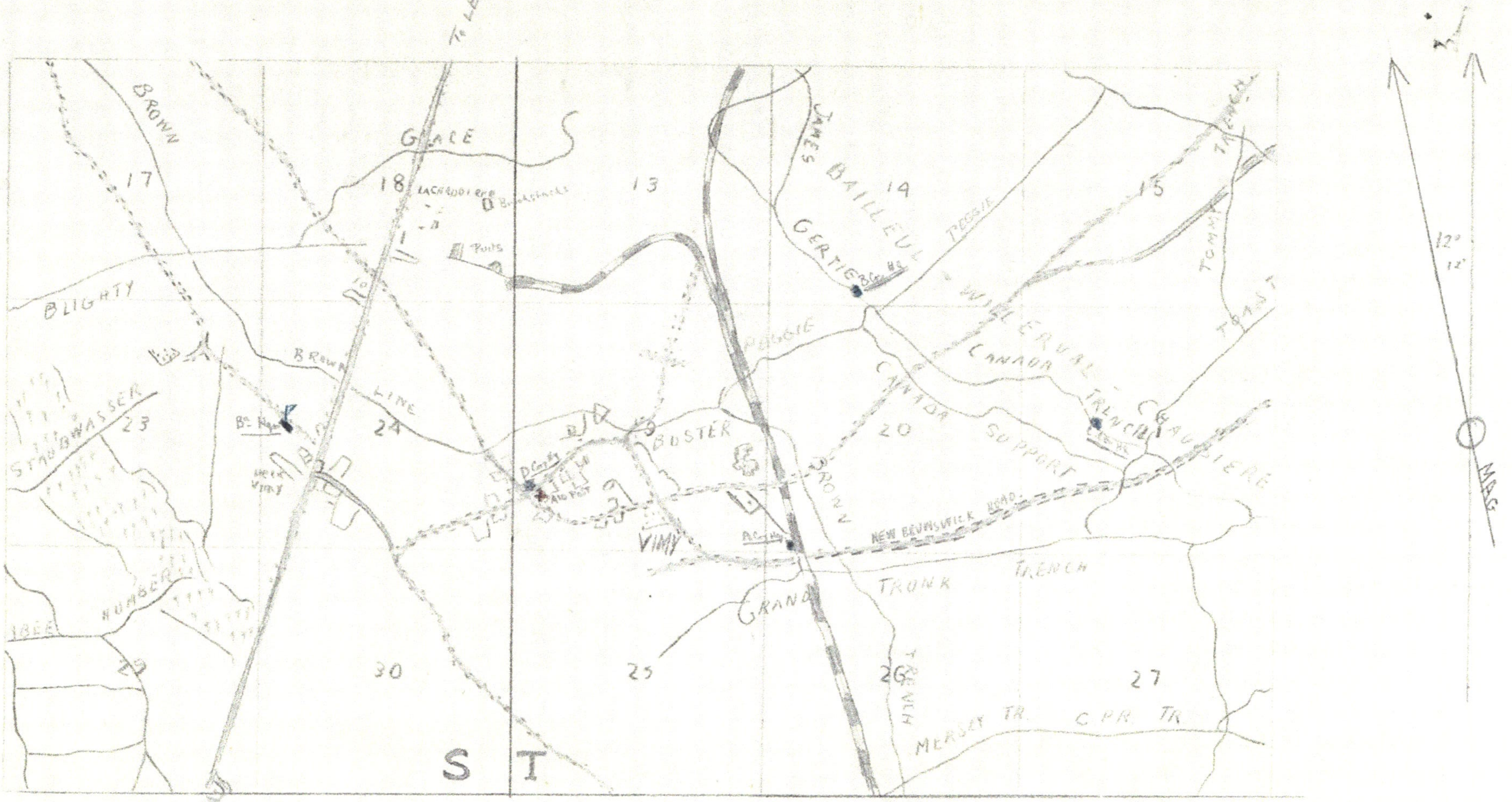

Map showing Disposition of Coys. while Bn in Reserve ~~in~~ VIMY—NOVA-SCOTIA area

To LENS
To ARRAS
MAG
12°
12'
BROWN
GRACE
BLIGHTY
BROWN LINE
STAUBWASSER
HUMBER
JAMES
BAILLEUL
GERTIE
POGGIE
WILLERVAL
CANADA TRENCH
CANADA SUPPORT
TOMMY TRENCH
TOAST
SAUCIERE
BUSTER
BROWN
NEW BRUNSWICK ROAD
TRUNK TRENCH
GRAND
TRENCH
MERSEY TR.
C.P.R. TR.
VIMY
LACHRODIERE
Puits
Bn Hqrs
D Coy
AID POST
17
18
13
14
15
23
24
20
29
30
25
26
27
S
T

App 3

Ref Map MARQUEUIL 1/20000

The following redistribution of Battalion will take place

The line at present held by three Companies will now be held by four Companies which are practically equal. Each Coy. will have (A) ½ Platoon in Observation & S.O.S Line.

(B) 1½ Platoons in 1st Battn Line & S.O.S

(C) 2 Platoons in 2nd Battn Line & main Line of Resistance

A MONTREAL - QUEBEC - LILY ELSIE Trenches
B TEDDIE GERRARD - NEW BRUNSWICK Trenches
C GERTIE - CANADA - KURTON Trenches

"A" Coy front will be as follows
ACHEVILLE Rd exclusive to 150 Yds N. of TEASER TRENCH in NEW BRUNSWICK TRENCH with a post in Observation.
(1) Line in MONTREAL TRENCH at Junction of TOPER TRENCH with MONTREAL and in CANADA & KURTON LINE from ACHEVILLE Rd exclusive to the bend in CANADA TRENCH 300 Yds S. of A in CANADA

C. Coy Front will be from 150 Yds N. of TEASER TRENCH to TOAST TRENCH exclusive in NEW BRUNSWICK TRENCH with a post in QUEBEC TRENCH at the Junction of
(2) TORQUAY with QUEBEC,
and in CANADA & KURTON LINE from a point 300 Yds S. of A in CANADA to MERICOURT Rd inclusive

B Coy front will be as follows, from TOAST TRENCH inclusive
(3) to TOMMY TRENCH exclusive in TEDDIE GERRARD LINE with a post at the Junction of TOAST TRENCH & LILY ELSIE and in CANADA LINE & KURTON LINE from MERICOURT Rd exclusive to PEGGY TRENCH inclusive

"D" Coy front will be as follows TOMMY TRENCH inclusive to VESTA TILLEY exclusive in TEDDIE GERRARD LINE with
(4) a post at the junction of LILY ELSIE with TOMMY TRENCH and in CANADA LINE from PEGGY TRENCH exclusive to Junction of JAMES & GERTIE.

Company Commanders will reconnoitre their new positions and be ready to occupy them immediately on the order being given — A taking over the posts from C. Coy and B + D. Coys adjusting their boundaries.

No movement to CANADA TRENCH will take place until 1st Battn + Observation Line have been adjusted when the two Platoons of A + C. Coys will proceed to CANADA VIA TOAST TRENCH + those of B + D. Coys VIA PEGGIE.

This redistribution will take place tomorrow commencing at 10. A.M.

Ref. Para. 1. A. Coy will hold two posts in Observation Line each consisting of 1 Section, a post presently occupied by No 1 post C Coy about T.17.c.3.3. and 1 Section at post already mentioned in Para. 1.

B. Coy will hold 2 Posts in Observation + S.O.S. LINE each Post to consist of 1 Section.

One Post will be at Junction of TWIST with QUEBEC and one at junction of TWIST with LILY ELSIE

This will make the allocation as follows:

A. Coy will have two Posts each of one Section
B. " " " " one Section
C " " " 1 Post of ½ Platoon
D " " " 1 Post of ½ Platoon
} all in Observation and S.O.S. LINE

__Headquarters will be situated as follows__

Battn H.Q. at T.20.c.2.1 (Old A. Coy H.qrs [illegible])
D. Coy will remain in their present H.Q.
C Coy will occupy present Battn H.Q.
A. Coy will take over from 7th S.R. in CANADA
B. Coy " GERTIE.

C. Coy will be responsible for all Stores at present at Battn H.Q. + will hand them over to incoming unit

T. Drummond Shiels
Capt + Adj
1/4 Royal Scots.
Qen,

WAR DIARY

JUNE, 1918

App. 4.

Strength Figures

Additions to Strength

	O.	O.R.
New Drafts	5	97
From hospital	1	79
" leave to U.K.	-	4
" Trade Test	-	1
" duty as Q.M.S. 156 Bde Hqrs.	-	1
Re-posted to 1/4 R.S. from 1/8th Sco Rif.	-	4
	6	186

Deductions from Strength

	O.	O.R.
To hospital	4	148
Killed	-	1
Wounded " accidentally		6,
To Cadet Unit, U.K.	-	3
" Military Prison	-	1
Re-classfd at Base	-	8
	4	168

Strength of Bn. on 30.6.18

	O.	O.R.
With Bn.	31	701
Bde. Pioneer Co.	-	22
" "Pool of Sigs."	-	4
" Hqrs. Runners	-	2
Courses of Instm.	5	25
Leave to U.K.	3	51
Base for Re-classfn.	-	3
In hosp. (under 4 days) O.R.	4	14
"Sundry" detached	3	46
	46	844

"Died of Wounds" during the month

1 Officer & 1 O.R.

(previously shown - in May - as "Wounded")

Attached (not included above)

	O.	O.R.
Medical Offr	1	-
R.C. Chaplain	1	-
A.O.C. S/Sgt. (at present at Div. Arm. Workshop)		1
	2	1

VR 4

Confidential

War Diary

of

1/4 Bn The Royal Scots (Q.R.)

from 1st to 31st July 1918

Vol. XXXVIIII

Instructions regarding War Diaries and Intelligence Summaries are contained in F. S. Regs., Part II. and the Staff Manual respectively. Title Pages will be prepared in manuscript.

WAR DIARY
or
INTELLIGENCE SUMMARY

(Erase heading not required.)

Army Form C. 2118

1/4th Bn The Royal Scots

Place	Date	Hour	Summary of Events and Information — July — Page 1	Remarks and references to Appendices
			Ref. Map. MAROEUIL 1/20,000	
HILLS CAMP NEUVILLE ST VAAST. July 1	1	—	Battalion left billetting area at 7-30 am & proceeded to a field on ST ELOI – CAMBLAIN L'ABBÉ Road near OTTAWA CAMP to be inspected along with the remainder of 152nd Inf Bde by H.R.H. The Duke of Connaught. The Bde was drawn up in open square. This Bn being on the Right Flank 7th Royal Scots in centre & 7th Scottish Rifles on left flank. The Bde received His Royal Highness with the Royal salute & after being inspected, the 4th Royal Scots were ordered to march past in column of route. The men were particularly steady & HRH expressed his satisfaction at their smart & soldierlike bearing (see app 1.)	TDW. App 1.
	5th–7th		The Battalion took part in competitions organised by the Bde & did very creditably gaining 4 first & 2 seconds in Rifle meeting, 2 Firsts in Signalling, 2 in Horse Show, 2nd in Cooks competition.	TDW
	8th		The Bn took over centre subsection of the Right Section of 52nd Div Front (App 2 O.O. 13). from 4th K.O.S.B.	App 2
	8th–14th		This sector has been fairly quiet as far as enemy shelling. Our artillery have been active & caused the enemy great discomfort. On the 9th a Hun plane was brought down in our section at BROWN LINE by one of our "fighters", the plane burst into flames when about 30 feet from the ground, the pilot being killed before it crashed. The plane	TDW

1875 Wt. W593/826 1,000,000 4/15 J.B.C. & A. A.D.S.S./Forms/C. 2118.

Instructions regarding War Diaries and Intelligence Summaries are contained in F. S. Regs., Part II. and the Staff Manual respectively. Title Pages will be prepared in manuscript.

WAR DIARY
or
INTELLIGENCE SUMMARY
(Erase heading not required.)

Army Form C. 2118

Place	Date	Hour	Summary of Events and Information — July. Page 2	Remarks and references to Appendices
Centre Sub-Section of Right Section 52nd Div Front	7-14 contd		was completely destroyed by fire & the pilot's body was badly charred. He was buried beside his plane. The usual patrols were sent out, with the object of identification, but no enemy were seen. News received that 50th Canadian Inf Battalion would take over our sector from HOME TRENCH to WESTERN Rd. occupied by A & C Coys. 9th Royal Scots took over from our B Coy their area from HUDSON & OTTAWA & EAST of it. D Coy in the BROWN Line would be relieved by the 47th Canadian Inf Bn on relief the Bn would move to the Right subsector of the Left section & take over the area occupied by the 6th H.L.I. (Appendix 3)	TWS App 3
Left Sub-Section of Right Section 52nd Div. Section	15th		The relief as mentioned above was carried out without incident & casualty the relief started about 4pm & the relief of the HLI was completed by 1 am on the 16th.	TWS
	16-17		Usual patrols sent out Enemy planes active & considerable artillery activity	TWS
	18-19		Quiet during day, considerable gas shelling round T25 between 12 midnight & 1 am. No casualties. H.Q. staff wore respirators for 2 hrs.	TWS
	20		Information received that Battn would be relieved by a Battn of 8th Division.	RBL
Lancaster Camp Mont St Eloy.	22		Battn relieved on 22 by 2nd Middlesex and on relief proceeded to Lancaster Camp. St Eloy for night 22/23	RBL

1875 Wt. W593/826 1,000,000 4/15 J.B.C. & A. A.D.S.S./Forms/C. 2118.

Army Form C. 2118

Instructions regarding War Diaries and Intelligence Summaries are contained in F. S. Regs., Part II. and the Staff Manual respectively. Title Pages will be prepared in manuscript.

WAR DIARY
or
INTELLIGENCE SUMMARY
(Erase heading not required.)

4 Battn The Royal Scots

Place	Date	Hour	July Summary of Events and Information Page 3	Remarks and references to Appendices
Mont St Eloy	23.		The Battn was inspected by Sir Aylmer Hunter Weston, the Corps Comdr. After the inspection the Corps Commander expressed his satisfaction of the appearance and smartness of the Battalion. He also addressed and shook hands with all Gallipoli veterans. After this the Battn marched	
Bois d' Olhain			to a camping ground in Bois d'Olhain at Q8d32 where it passed into G.H.Q reserve and was under four hours notice to move.	Sheet 44B. RBL.
	24 – 29.		The first day was devoted to rest and cleaning up. The Battalion then commenced a training programme of about four hours work per day. Four days per week were to be devoted to tactical training, platoon & Coy schemes, the remainder to specialist training, musketry, steady drill &c. This programme was much interfered with by heavy rain which turned the paths through the woods and camp into a quagmire. On Sunday 28 platoon schemes were successfully carried out on the ground between Bois	

Instructions regarding War Diaries and Intelligence Summaries are contained in F. S. Regs., Part II. and the Staff Manual respectively. Title Pages will be prepared in manuscript.

WAR DIARY
or
INTELLIGENCE SUMMARY
(Erase heading not required.)

Army Form C. 2118

4 Bn The Royal Scots

Place	Date	Hour	Summary of Events and Information	Remarks and references to Appendices
			July Page 4	
Bois d'Olhain	24 - 29		des Clercs and Point 170. Monday 29 was reserved as a day of rest and inter-Coy football matches also running jumping, bombing, + tug-of-war competitions were carried out.	Ref map France Sheet 44 B
			At noon a warning order was received from Brigade that on the 30th the Battn would move to MAROEUIL and the following day the Division would take over from the Canadian Division holding the left of the Canadian front (Arras) and an advance party was sent off to MAROEUIL to take over billets for the Battn.	PBL
		30.	The order received on 29th was afterwards amended — ECOIVRES being now the destination of the Battn. At 7.45 the Battn left camp and marched via VERDREL — LES 4 VENTS — CAMBLAIN L'ABBE to ECOIVRES where it was quartered in hutments, near cross roads at F15 a 0 6, about 12 am. The Commanding Officer + Adjutant preceding ahead of the Battn. by motor lorry to reconnoitre the line to be taken up, on 31st inst. See Appendix I a	Ref. map 1/40000 Sheets 36 b and 51 C
ECOIVRES.				PBL.

Army Form C. 2118

Instructions regarding War Diaries and Intelligence Summaries are contained in F. S. Regs., Part II. and the Staff Manual respectively. Title Pages will be prepared in manuscript.

WAR DIARY
or
INTELLIGENCE SUMMARY
(Erase heading not required.)

4/4 Battn. The Royal Scots Q.E.R.

Place	Date	Hour	Summary of Events and Information	Remarks and references to Appendices
			July. Page 5.	
ECOIVRES	31		At 5.30 am orders were received from Bde for the relief by this Battn. of the 87 Canadian Infantry Battn. The Brigade relieving the 11 Canadian Infantry Bde – 7th R Scots relieving the Left Battn in the Front System. 7th Cameronians, the Right Battn in the Front System and 4th R. Scots, the Support Battn in the BROWN LINE.	Ref Map MAROEUIL 1/20 000
			At 9.45 am the Battn left camp and marched to MADAGASCAR CORNER (A26d83) where a halt was made for mid-day meal in open ground at G3a + d at 12 am. Thereafter the Battn moved through ECURIE to ROCLINCOURT where guides from the outgoing Battn were met and the relief proceeded by daylight, half platoons moving at 100 yd intervals, Coys at 500 yd intervals. Relief was completed by 6.45 pm. There were 5 men slightly wounded by enemy shelling and 4 men sent to hospital suffering from effects of enemy gas. See Appendix II.	RBb Ref Map 51B NW 1/20 000 App II a
Support Battn. Hqrs B27c70.10			The Battn took over the dispositions of the 87 Canadian Battn. as shown on attached sketch map. A re adjustment of the Southern + Northern Boundaries of the Brigade sub-sector of defence necessitated plans being made for a redistribution to be carried out on the 1st August.	Appendix III a

1875 Wt. W593/826 1,000,000 4/15 J.B.C. & A. A.D.S.S./Forms/C. 2118.

Instructions regarding War Diaries and Intelligence Summaries are contained in F. S. Regs., Part II. and the Staff Manual respectively. Title Pages will be prepared in manuscript.

WAR DIARY
or
INTELLIGENCE SUMMARY
(Erase heading not required.)

4/ Battn The Royal Scots Q&R

Army Form C. 2118

Place	Date	Hour	Summary of Events and Information — July — Page 6	Remarks and references to Appendices
Support Bn Hqrs B27c70.10	31.		Enemy artillery has not been active since the Battn took over. Desultory Shelling with occasional ~~battery~~ concentrated fire from enemy 5·9's on Railway Cutting about B27a, a small quantity of gas shells of unidentified type were mixed with the HEs.	Ref Map 51B. NW 1/20000. RRb
			General. The health of the Battn throughout the month has been good. Strength + reinforcement state for the month is attached	App. IVa
			P. Bristowe Carr Lt. a/adj 4/Bn The Royal Scots Q&R.	

1875 Wt. W593/826 1,000,000 4/15 J.B.C. & A. A.D.S.S./Forms/C. 2118.

SPECIAL ORDER OF THE DAY

by

appendix I

MAJOR GENERAL J. HILL C.B. D.S.O. COMMANDING 52nd (Lowland) DIV

3rd July 1918

The following message which has been received from General Officer Commanding VIIIth Army Corps is published for the information of all ranks.

"Field Marshal His Royal Highness the Duke of Connaught was much pleased with the parade of the 156 Infantry Brigade of the 52nd Lowland Division yesterday , and desired that his pleasure at meeting again, in so far different a theatre of War, the fine Division, under the command of MAJOR GENERAL JOHN HILL C.B. D.S.O., that he had seen only three months ago in PALESTINE, should be conveyed to all ranks.

He was struck by the healthy, resolute and smart appearance of the men on parade, and was pleased both with the excellence of their first"present" and by the good march discipline and soldierly bearing displayed by those officers, men and transport that marched past him.

He will let His Majesty the King know that he has in the 52nd a Division that will worthily uphold the honour of their King and Country.

The Corps Commander, Sir Aylmer Hunter-Weston, congratulates General LEGGETT'S Brigade, and the whole Division on the high praise given it by Field Marshal His Royal Highness The Duke of Connaught, the King's Uncle.

The Corps Commander is sure that the Officers and men of the Division are determined to devote every minute of their time to improving their discipline, training, and therefore, their fighting power, so as to continue to be a credit to SCOTLAND and to justify the high reputation that the Division has already made for itself."

Sd. C. G. Maude,
Lieut. Colonel.
A.A. & Q.M.G. 52nd (Lowland) Division.

SECRET. Copy No....11...

Appendix II

1/4th. Bn. The Royal Scots (Q.E.R.)

ORDER No. 13
by
Lieut-Colonel A. Maclaine Mitchell, D.S.O., Comdg.

- -

Ref. Map MAROEUIL 1/20,000. 6th. July, 1918.

1. The 156th. Inf. Bde. will relieve the 155th. Inf. Bde. in the Right Section of the 52nd. Divisional Sector on the 8th/9th. July, 1918.

2. Reliefs will take place as follows:-

July 8th. 1/7th. Sco. Rifles will relieve 1/5th. R.S.F. in the Right Sub-section.
1/4th. Royal Scots " " 1/4th. K.O.S.B. in the Centre Sub-section.
1/7th. Royal Scots " " 1/4th. R.S.F. in the Left Sub-Section.

3. On July 7th., the 4th. R.S. will send the following advance parties to the line:-
Bn. I.O., 1 Officer per Coy., 1 N.C.O. per Platoon, 2 Bn. Runners, 2 runners per Coy., 2 Bn. Signallers, Bn. Scout N.C.O., 1 Lewis Gun N.C.O. per Coy., Bn. and Coy. Gas NCO's.
They will be met at 9.15 a.m. by guides from the Coys. they are relieving, at Right Brigade Hqrs. A.6.c.8.5.

4. On the 8th. July, guides from Bn. H.Q., Coy. H.Q., and Platoons of the 4th. K.O.S.B. will be waiting at A.11.a.4.7. from 9.15 till 10 a.m. to conduct the Battalion to the line.

5. The Battalion will march as follows:-

"A" Company	starting at	8	a.m.
"B" "	"	" 8.15	"
"C" "	"	" 8.30	"
"D" "	"	" 8.45	"
Bn. Hqrs.	"	" 8.15	"

There will be 200 yards between Companies and a similar distance between platoons.

6. WERNEY ALLEY will be the Communication Trench used by 4th. R.S.

7. The Bn. Lewis Gun officer will arrange for the exchange of L.G. magazines, cases, etc.

8. All existing communications, etc., will stand. Trench stores will be taken over and a receipt given. The original will be sent to Bn. Orderly Room 6 hours after relief. Great care must be taken over these returns.

9. Completion of relief will be reported by the code word "DANSON".

10. In the event of an enemy attack while relief is in progress, Coys. will assemble in the nearest defences and report to the nearest Bn. Commander or Brigade Hqrs.

11. Details not proceeding to the line will move to Divl. Reception Camp by 2 p.m. on 8th. July. Transport will be brigaded at LATTA CAMP at 2 p.m. on 8th. July.

12. Bn. Hqrs. will close at present camp at 11 a.m. and re-open at same hour at T.26.d.4.3.

13. Acknowledge.

T. Drummond Watson
Capt. & Adjt.,
1/4th. Royal Scots (Q.E.R.)

Issued at.....9 pm.....

SECRET. Copy No......9..

1/4th. Bn. The Royal Scots (Q.E.R.)

Appendix Ia

ORDER No. 17
by
Lieut-Colonel A. Maclaine Mitchell, D.S.O., Comdg.

- -

29th. July, 1918.

1. The 52nd. Division is relieving the Canadian Division at present holding the Left Sub-Sector of the Canadian Corps Front (ARRAS Sector).

2. Relieve will probably commence on night 31st. July/1st. Aug.

3. As a preliminary move, the 156th. Bde. Group will proceed by route march to MAROEUIL on the 30th. inst. On arrival they will go into billets and camps.

4. An advance party of 2/Lieut. A. W. Philp and 1 N.C.O. from B, C and D Coys. will report at Bn. H.Q. at 1 p.m. today with cycles and rations until midnight tomorrow. There-after they will report at H.Q., 7th. Royal Scots at 1.15 p.m.

5. Further orders will be issued later.

P Bonstowe Carre

Issued at...12.20 pm...

Lieut. & A/Adjt.,
1/4th. Royal Scots (Q.E.R.)

Distribution:-

Copy No.	
1	C.O.
2	Office.
3	"A" Coy.
4	"B" "
5	"C" "
6	"D" "
7	T.O.
8	Q.M.
9	Adjt.
10	R.S.M.
11	H.Q. Mess.
12	War Diary.

War Diary

SECRET. Copy No....12.....

1/4th. Bn. The Royal Scots (Q.R.R.)

ORDER No. 18
by
Lieut-Colonel A. Maclaine Mitchell, D.S.O., Comdg.

Appendix Ia

- -

Ref. Map 1/40,000 Sheets 36b and 51c. 29th. July, 1918.

1. RELIEF.
The 52nd. Lowland Division is relieving 4th. Canadian Division in the Left Sub-section of the ARRAS sector on the night 31st. July/1st. Aug. 1918. and subsequent days.

2. MOVE.
4th. Royal Scots will move to camp or billets at ECOIVRES.
Order of march :-
Hqrs., D,C,B,A Coys., Bde. Hqrs.
The Bn. will fall in on the road ready to move at 7-45am.
Route:- Brigade starting point at Q.14.b.2.6. - VERDREL - FRESNICOURT - road junction F.30.a.6.4. - LES 4 VENTS - CAMBLAIN L'ABBE - ECOIVRES.

3. Reveille will be at 5-30 a.m., Sick Parade 5-30 a.m. and breakfast 6 a.m. tomorrow.

4. TRANSPORT.
Transport will march with the Battalion.

5. DISTANCES ON MARCH.
100 yds. between Companies. Transport 100 yds. from Battn.
4th. Royal Scots lead the Brigade Column.

6. DRESS.
Fighting order with Balmorals. Steel helmets will be carried on the right shoulder. Waterproof sheets will be carried on the men.

7. ADVANCE PARTIES will meet Coys. at White House, MONT ST. ELOI and guide them to their camp or billets. Coys. will report their arrival in camp to Bn. H.Q. by code word "MUDDY".

8. SUPPLIES.
Rations for the 31st. will be carried in the supply wagons of the train.

9. BAGGAGE ARRANGEMENTS.
Men's packs with great-coats inside will be stacked on road-side to the right of Guard Tent by 6-45 a.m. Canteen Stores, Orderly Room Stores, Band stores and rifles, Signalling Stores and H.Q. surplus mess stores will be dumped at same place and same time as men's packs. Officer's valises will be stacked on road-side near Officers' lines by 7 a.m.

10. MEDICAL.
1 Ambulance wagon will call at Bn. Aid Post by 7-30 a.m. to collect any sick for evacuation.

11. The camp will be left scrupulously clean.

12. Bn. Hqrs. will close at present camp at 7-45 a.m. and re-open at ECOIVRES on arrival.

13. Marching out states will be rendered to Orderly Room by 7 a.m.

14. ACKNOWLEDGE.

P. Bristowe Carr

Issued at...9:30 pm...

Lieut. & A/Adjt.,
1/4th. Royal Scots (Q.R.R.)

SECRET. Copy No..1.....

appendix IIa

1/4th. Bn. The Royal Scots (Q.E.R.)

ORDER No. 19
by
Lieut-Colonel A. Maclaine Mitchell, D.S.O., Comdg.

- -

Ref. Map MAROEUIL 1/20,000. **31st. July, 1918.**

1. The 4th. Royal Scots will relieve the 87th. Canadian Inf. Bn. today and will, as far as possible, take over the present dispositions of that unit.

2. Advance parties as detailed separately will be met by guides at ROCLINCOURT cross roads.

c3. The Bn. will fall in close to men's lines at 9.30 a.m. markers at 9-15 a.m. and will proceed by march route in the following order:- Hqrs., "A", "D", "B" "C" Coys., moving off at 9-45 a.m. via cross roads at F.15.a.0.6. passing these at 10 a.m., then via cross roads at A.8.a.5.7. - LENS-ARRAS Road as far as MADAGASCAR CORNER A.26.d.8.3. where a halt will be made for midday meal in open space at G.3.a. & c. Thereafter the Bn. will move through ECURIE and ROCLINCOURT.

4. Guides. Guides from the 87th. Canadian Bn. will meet the Bn. at ROCLINCOURT at 1.30 p.m.

5. Safety precautions. The usual intervals will be maintained on line of march until ROCLINCOURT, after which, 500 yds. distance. All movement East of BROWN LINE will be by trenches.

6. Action in case of attack. In event of an attack takingplace during relief, the Bn. will man the nearest defences and report to the Hqrs. of the unit it is relieving giving their location. They will also send an officer with the above information to Bde. Hqrs.

7. Handing over. All maps, aeroplane photos, schemes, log books, tables of work, trench stores, etc., will be taken over. Receipts for above will be forwarded to Bn. Hqrs. not later than 18 hours after completion of relief.

8. Completion of relief will be reported to Bn. Hqrs. by code word "GINGER".

9. As soon as possible after taking over, all Companies will send a map to Bn. Hqrs. shewing dispositions in line by platoons and sections. Lewis Gun sections will be shewn differently to rifle sections.

10. ACKNOWLEDGE.

P Bristowe Carr

Issued at...7 am.......

Lieut. & A/Adjt.,
1/4th. Royal Scots (Q.E.R.

Distribution:-

Copy No.		No.	
1	C.O.	7	Q.M.
2	Office	8	T.O.
3	"A" Coy.	9	Adjt.
4	"B" "	10	R.S.M.
5	"C" "	11	H.Q. Mess
6	"D" "	12	War Diary
7			

Appendix "III"

DISPOSITION SKETCH

BATTALION.............. DATE..............

11TH CDN. INF. BDE. 27-7-18

REF. SHEET 51B N.W.

— Bn HQ
— Coy HQ
— L.G. Post
— Platoon area
— A Coy
— B Coy
— C Coy
— D Coy

TOMMY ALLEY
OUSE ALLEY
OUSE SIDING
BOW
OUSE ALLEY
SUPPORT
TRENCH
BAILLEUL EAST
NORTH TYNE ALLEY
TYNE ALLEY
HARROWGATE POST
BOLTON ABBEY
ZEHNER ALLEY
BRIERLEY HILL
BACK TRENCH
BAILLEUL
BAILLEUL ALLEY
RAILWAY POST
RAILWAY ALLEY
GULLY POST
GULLY
3 Sect.
Coy HQ
1 Platoon + 1 sect.
1 A.A.L.G.
GAUL POST
FRED ALLEY
LOCALITY
POST TR.
BAILLEUL POST
KILKERRAN
KILKERRAN TR.
KAY ALLEY
THAMES ALLEY
TRENCH
GREEN
Bn HQ
FOLLY TR.
TOWY ALLEY
THAMES
SUPPORT ALLEY
MISSOURI TR.
MACK TR.
TRIPOLI TR.
BROWN
1 A.A.L.G.
Coy HQ
TONGUE POST
CHANTICLER SWITCH
TUSK TRENCH
ALLEN TR.
20
22
23
26
27
28
29
2
3
4
5
B
H

WAR DIARY JULY 1918 1/4 Royal Scots (Q.R.)

Additions to Strength

	Off	OR
From Hospital	-	89
Reinforcements from UK etc.	1	126
From duty at Corps Hdqrs EEF (previously struck off)	-	1
From Detention Barracks Cairo	-	1
	1	217

Deductions from Strength

	Off	OR
To Hospl (sick)		62
" (now over 7 days)		17
" Cadet Unit UK as candidates for Comm	-	4
medically reclassified at the Base		2
Lieut Cass to UK to resume medical studies	1	-
A/Capt W.S. Ferrier Invalided to UK	1	-
To 156 Bde TM Batty	-	1
" M.G. Battn	-	1
Wounded	-	6
"		5
	2	98

Strength of Battalion 31/7/18

	Offrs	OR
With Battalion	17	579
Battalion Hdqrs	6	95
Administrative Portion	3	57
Nucleus "	1	34
Transport	1	56
att Bde Transport		2
Bde Hdqrs Runners & Scouts		5
" Guard		8
S.A.A. Dump "		13
1st Army Rest Camp		5
Courses of Instruction	3	13
Leave to UK	7	54
Detached	2	41
Absent without Leave		1
In Hospital (sick) (O.Rs under 7 days)	5	20
Reinforcements at Reception Camp	-	10
	45	993

Attached (not included above)

	Off	OR
M.O.	1	-
R.C. Chaplain	1	-
	2	-

Appendix IVa

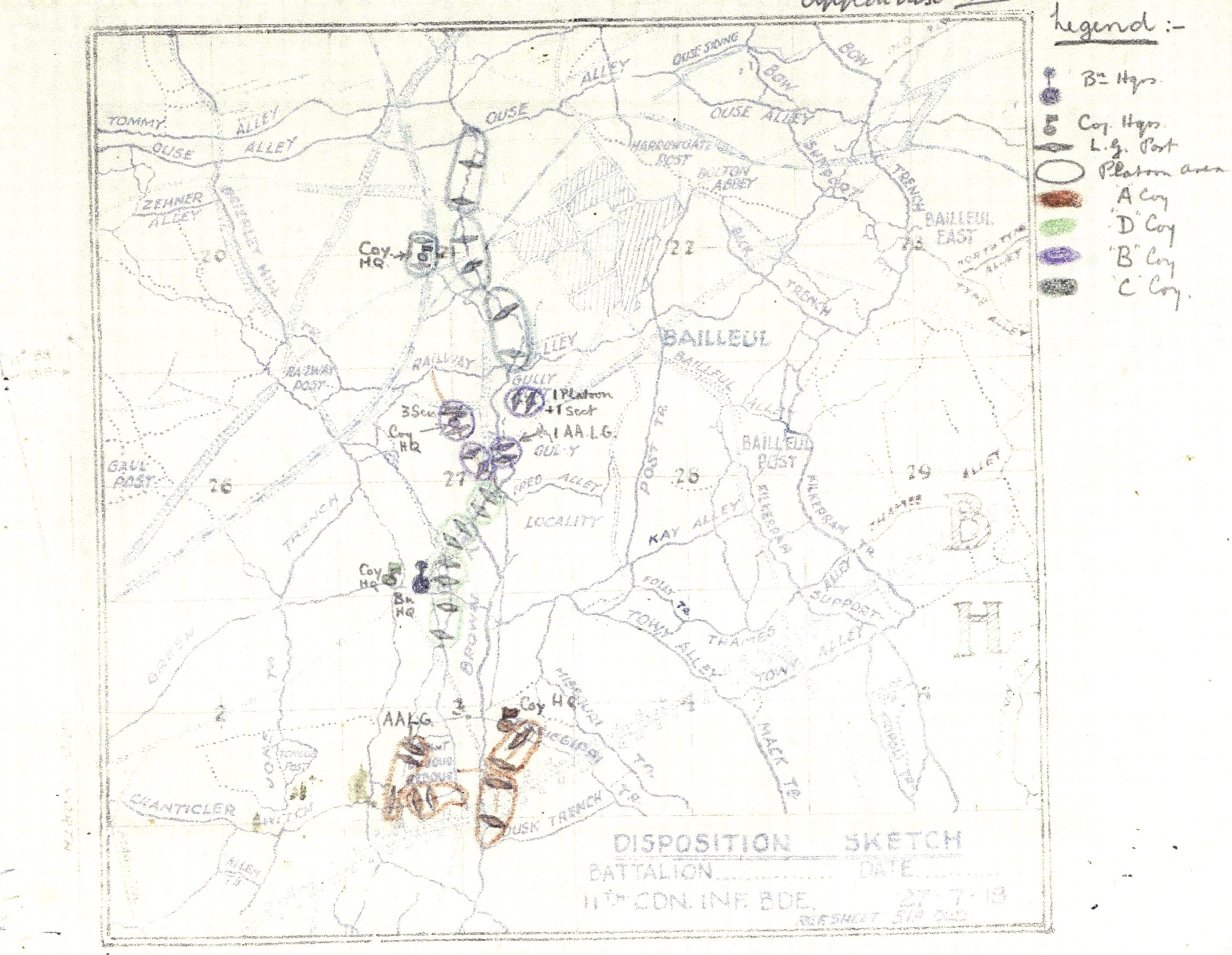
Legend :-
Bn Hqrs
Coy. Hqrs
L.G. Post
Platoon area
'A' Coy
'D' Coy
'B' Coy
'C' Coy
DISPOSITION SKETCH
BATTALION .... DATE ....
11th CON. INF. BDE. 27. 7. 18
REF. SHEET 51B
TOMMY ALLEY
OUSE ALLEY
ZEHNER ALLEY
BRIERLEY HILL TR.
OUSE SIDING
BOW
HARROWGATE POST
BOLTON ABBEY
SUPPORT TRENCH
BAILLEUL EAST
BACK TRENCH
BAILLEUL
BAILLEUL POST
RAILWAY
RAILWAY POST
GULLY
GAUL POST
FRED ALLEY
LOCALITY
POST TR.
KAY ALLEY
KILKERRAN
FOLLY TR.
TOWN ALLEY
THAMES
MACK TR.
TRIPOLI TR.
MISSOURI TR.
DUSK TRENCH
CHANTICLER
ALLEN TR.
GREEN
20
21
22
25
26
27
29
Coy HQ
3 Sect
1 Platoon +1 Sect
1 AA.L.G.
Bn HQ
AA.L.G.

Secret. Bn. Order No. 14 Appendix III

Copy No. [illegible]

[illegible] 14th July 1918.

(1) The 4th Canadian Division is relieving the portion of the 52 Division, S. of WESTERN Rd. at junc. B.2.a.08 thence due West to junction of MERSEY Alley & Railway embankment thence to A.12.a.8.5.

(2)(a) On the 15 July the 50 Canadian Inf. Bn. will relieve A & C Coy. of 4th Royal Scots East of & including the BLACK LINE.

(b) C Coy. 47th Can. Inf. Bn. will relieve 'D' Coy at present in BROWN LINE

(c) Relief will commence approx at 2.30 pm.

(3) On relief the 4th Royal Scots will relieve the 6th H.L.I. in the Right Sub-section of the Left Section of the Divisional Sector.

The 8th Sco. Rifles will relieve 'B' Coy. in the BROWN LINE between MERSEY Alley & NEW BRUNSWICK Rd.

(4) 6 Guides will be arranged by the Scout officer for platoons in BLACK & BLUE LINE to meet 50th Canadian Bn. at Commandant's House B.7.d.6.2. at 2 pm.

He will also arrange for 1 guide to be at LONGWOOD Rly. Embankment (B.13.a.10.65) at 1.30 pm to guide C Coy. 47 Canadian Bn. to junction of WILLERVAL & FARBUS Rd. where they will be met by 2 guides to be arranged for by D Coy.

(5) All maps Defence Schemes & Log Books will be handed over.

(6) Completion of relief will be reported by code word "HOUSE".
Present Bn. HQ. will be handed over to 7th Royal Scots.
Orders for our relief of the 6th HLI will follow later.

(7) Acknowledge.

Issued at 5-30 p.

14/7/18

T Drummond ...
Capt. & Adjt
4th Royal Scots (QER)

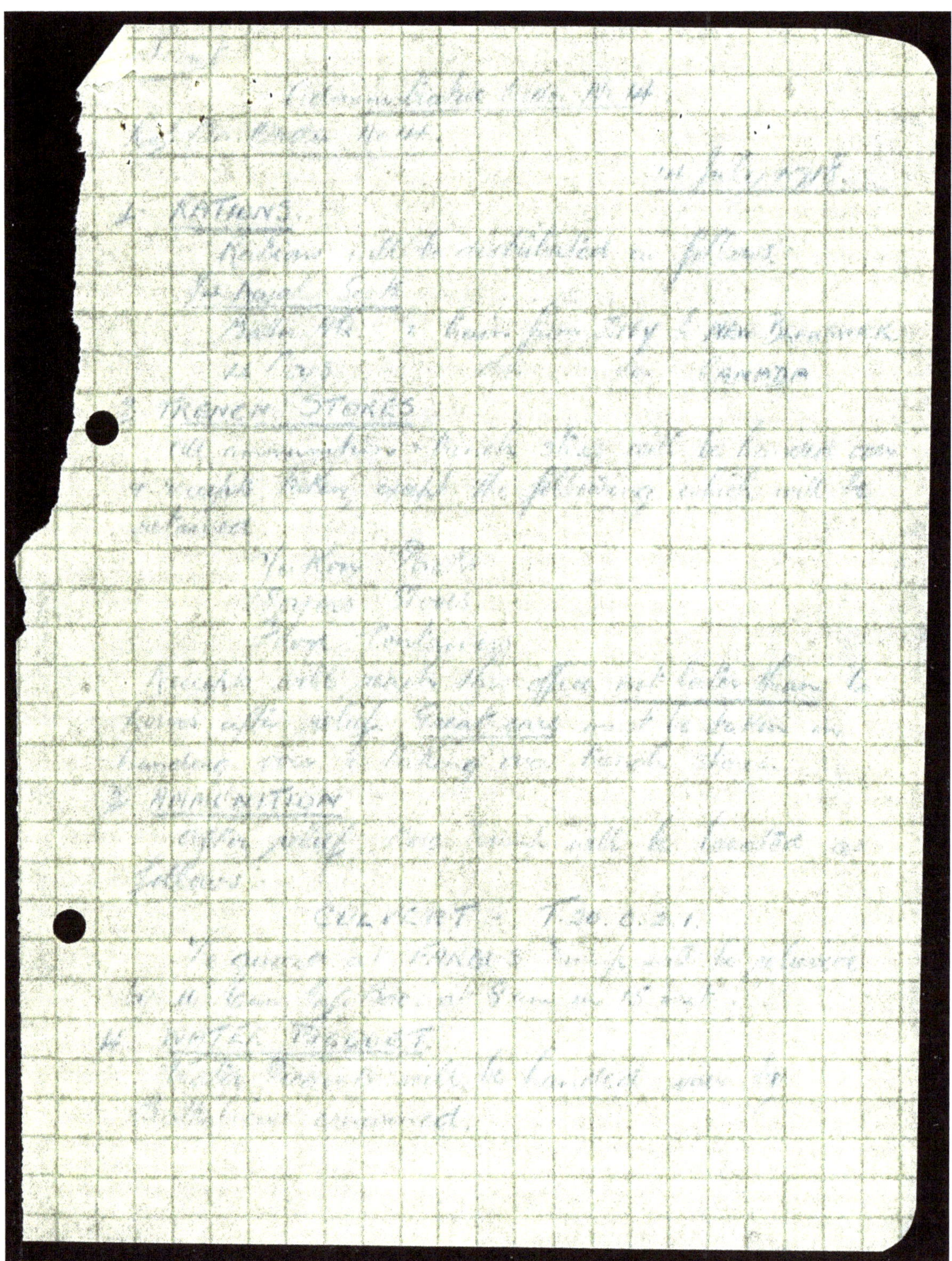

Administrative Order No. 44

[illegible]

14 July 1918.

1. RATIONS.

Rations will be distributed as follows:

For night [illegible]

Bn. HQ & [illegible] from [illegible] [illegible]

[illegible]

2. TRENCH STORES

All ammunition & trench stores will be handed over & receipts taken except the following which will be retained:

Very Light Pistols

Signal Stores

[illegible]

Receipts will reach this office not later than 6 hours after relief. Great care must be taken in handing over & taking over trench stores.

3. AMMUNITION

After relief [illegible] will be located as follows:

CULVERT – T.20.c.2.1.

The guard at [illegible] dump will be relieved by the [illegible] at 9 am on 15 inst.

4. WATER [illegible]

[illegible] will be handed over on relief [illegible] completed.

5. MEDICAL

Separate orders will be issued.

6. Acknowledge.

Issued at 0645 hrs

[illegible]

Capt & Adjt

2 Royal [illegible] [illegible]

ADMINISTRATIVE ORDER No.19
by
Lieut-Colonel A. Maclaine Mitchell,D.S.O., Comdg. *[handwritten:] adj Appendix IIa*

- -

31st. July, 1918.

1. SUPPLIES.
Refilling Point - F.20.b.2.8.
Rations will be delivered by 52nd. Div. Train to unit's transport lines.
Distribution. Battalions deliver from Q.M.Stores to Light Rly. ROCLINCOURT by 1st.Line Transport by 8 p.m. daily. From there supplies go forward by Light Rly. to the Support Bn. to B.27.a.1.4. If supplies go forward by ~~xxxxxxxxxxxxxxxxxxxxxxxxxxxx~~ Horse Transport to the support Bn. the route is ROCLINCOURT, CHANTICLER CORNER and BALEK Road.

2. WATER.
(a) There are 2 pipes running into the Section area, one on the extreme right and one on the left, and water is available at the following points:-

H.9.b.10.85	(In EFFIE TRENCH.)
H.9.b.3.3.	(in " ")
H.1.d.20.45.	(BLANCHE POST)
B/30.b.1.9.	
B.21.a.6.0.	
B.21.a.8.3.	
B.21;a.6.8.	

The Support Bn. should bring all water forward by Light Rly. or Transport.
Water Picquets will be taken over by Battalion concerned.

3. TRANSPORT.
The Transport Lines and Q.M.Stores will be taken over today and tomorrow from the 87th. Canadian Bn. at A.26.c.9.1.
The Nucleus and Administrative Portion of the Bn. will move from present camp under orders to be issued by the Asst/Adjt.

4. LEWIS GUNS.
200 L.G.Drums per Bn. will be left in the line and the Bn. will deliver the same number of drums (less boxes and carriers) to the transport camp of the Bn. being relieved today reporting completion to Bn.Hqrs.

5. YUKON PACKS.
All Yukon Packs in possession will be taken to the trenches.

6. AMMUNITION.
(a) Brigade Dump (CAMPBELLS DUMP); B.20.a.4.8.
(b) Support Bn. Dump - B.27.c.7.0.

7. R.E.MATERIAL.
Main Dump - ROCLINCOURT. Advanced Dump -B.26.c;1.1.

8. SALVAGE.
Divl. Salvage Dump - ROCLINCOURT A.29.c.8.3. Position of Bn. Salvage Dump will be notified later. All salvage collected will be sent to Divl. Dump by Light Rly. or Horse Transport.

9. MEDICAL.
Support Battalion - B.27.c;6.6. RELAY POST - B.20.d.1.9.

10. BURIAL.
The following cemetries are available:-
ROCLINCOURT - A.29.c.1.5. ANZIN - G.1.d.7.2.
MAROEUIL - F.27.a.9.5.
Bodies will be sent back by Light Rly., advising Bn.H/Q.

11. ACKNOWLEDGE.

[signature]

Lieut. & A/Adjt.,
1/4th. Royal Scots (Q.E.R.)

CONFIDENTIAL

Vol 5

WAR DIARY

1/4 BN. THE ROYAL SCOTS (QER)

FROM AUG. 1st to AUG. 31st 1918

VOLUME XXXIX.

Instructions regarding War Diaries and Intelligence Summaries are contained in F. S. Regs., Part II. and the Staff Manual respectively. Title Pages will be prepared in manuscript.

Vol XXXIX

WAR DIARY
or
INTELLIGENCE SUMMARY
(Erase heading not required.)

Army Form C. 2118

1/4 Battn The Royal Scots Q.R.

Place	Date	Hour	Summary of Events and Information	Remarks and references to Appendices
			August. Page I	
Support Bn Hq B27c71	1 –	6.	During the period 1 – 6 August several adjustments were made in the Brigade Boundaries necessitating readjustment of Defence Schemes and Coy Dispositions. The dispositions of the Battn on 6th August are shewn on "Amended Defence Scheme" (Appendix I Work was done in improving the fire positions in the BROWN LINE, in wiring and in draining of trenches, erecting and improving the camouflage on roads. A carrying party of 3 sections was provided nightly to the Right Line Battn. Thirty men per day were sent down to ROCLINCOURT to Bathe, the light railway providing transport. A regimental canteen was opened for the men near Battn. Hqrs. In order to give the men as much rest as possible before the Battn took over the line the BGC permitted 50% of the Battn to sleep without equipment and only 50% "stood to" morning & evening During the above period the enemy artillery was very inactive during the day, and only desultory shelling of the area occupied by the Battn occurred, the chief target being apparently our battery positions behind Bn. Hqrs. By night enemy artillery was more active and a large number of gas shells were thrown in the neighbourhood of the Railway Bridge (B27a.0.4.)	Ref map 51 B N/W 1/20000 Appendix I RBL

Instructions regarding War Diaries and Intelligence Summaries are contained in F. S. Regs., Part II. and the Staff Manual respectively. Title Pages will be prepared in manuscript.

Army Form C. 2118

WAR DIARY
or
INTELLIGENCE SUMMARY
(Erase heading not required.)

1/1 Bn The Royal Scots Q.E.R

Place	Date	Hour	Summary of Events and Information	Remarks and references to Appendices
			August. Page II	
Support Brn Hqrs B27c4.1	4th –	12th.	During this period much work was done on the defences. Fire bays were cut and fire positions improved. Barbed wire was put out in front of BROWN LINE and the existing trenches were improved. Three platoons were provided daily to the REs for work on the new Support Bn Hqrs at B27 a 2.5. On the 11th inst at 3.10 am. the S.O.S. rocket was observed on our Right and was repeated; our artillery opened an intense bombardment on the SOS lines to which the enemy replied but with much less density of fire. The intense fire lasted for about 15 minutes and then gradually slackened and eventually ceased. It transpired later that the call had come from H11b by reason of a raid on that area and had been repeated very far to the flank of the actual point of attack. On the same day the Commanding Officer Lieut Col A Maclaine Mitchell D.S.O. left the Battn for 14 days leave in U.K. his place being taken by Major J Mowat Slater. On the 12th at 1pm the enemy opened very heavy artillery fire with 4.2s on Battn Hqrs for 15 minutes a considerable quantity of irritant gas shells being mixed with the HEs. In all about 50 shells were thrown and then the enemy lengthened	Ref map 51B. NW. 1/20000

1875 Wt. W593/826 1,000,000 4/15 J.B.C. & A. A.D.S.S./Forms/C. 2118.

Instructions regarding War Diaries and Intelligence Summaries are contained in F. S. Regs., Part II. and the Staff Manual respectively. Title pages will be prepared in manuscript.

WAR DIARY
or
INTELLIGENCE SUMMARY.
(Erase heading not required.)

4Bn The Royal Scots QER

Army Form C. 2118.

Place	Date	Hour	Summary of Events and Information	Remarks and references to Appendices
			August. Page III	
Support Bn Hq.	Period		to Railway Cutting about B24a. Heavy counter battery fire was	
B24c 71	7th - 12		opened by our artillery by the order of 156 Bde.	
			Orders were received on the 12th for the relief on the 13th	PBL.
			of the 7th Royal Scots by this Bn in the Left Sub-section.	
	13th		The relief of the 7th Royal Scots by this Battn was carried	
			out by daylight. Relief was completed by 1600 without casualty.	PBL
			Orders for the move are attached. Appendix II.	Appendix II
	14th		Warning order received from 156 Inf Bde. ~~that~~ that 52 Division	
			would be relieved shortly by 51st Division. This Bde being relieved	PBL
			by 154 Bde relief to take place on the 15th or night 15/16.	
	16th		The relief took place today the 7th Argyll & Sutherland Highlanders being the	
			relieving unit. The relief did not take place until the evening (7.30pm).	TSW
			On relief the Bn proceeded by road to ECURIE Stn where it entrained on	
			the light Rly for SAVY, detraining there it proceeded to VILLERS, BRULIN &	
	17th		BRETONSART, being disposed as follows. HQ & A & B Coys at the former village	
			& C & D Coys & Transport at latter. HQ were established in a fine old chateau.	TSW
	17-18		These days were observed as rest days & reorganising generally.	
			The Division being in GHQ Reserve were in readiness to move at	TSW
			3 hrs notice	

D. D & L., London, E.C.
(A8004) Wt W1771/M2031 750,000 5/17 Sch. 52 Forms/C2118/14

Instructions regarding War Diaries and Intelligence Summaries are contained in F. S. Regs., Part II. and the Staff Manual respectively. Title Pages will be prepared in manuscript.

WAR DIARY
or
INTELLIGENCE SUMMARY
(Erase heading not required.)

1/4th Bn The Royal Scots

Army Form C. 2118

Place	Date	Hour	Summary of Events and Information — August 1918 — Page IV	Remarks and references to Appendices
	19-20		Platoon training was commenced & the Bn were also put through Gas.	TSW
	20th.		Orders received that Bn was to move to new billeting area at LATTRE ST QUENTIN. The Bn concentrated at the Chateau & moved off shortly after 11 pm & proceeded by TILLOY LES HERMAVILLE - crossroads N of 2nd O in NOYELLES-VION - Rd junction at L of LATTRE ST QUENTIN, where guides were waiting to conduct to billets. Owing to no room being at last named place, the Bn had to move on to WANQUENTIN, where billets were provided	Ref Map LENS 1/100000. TSW
WANQUENTIN	21st		The men were very tired & several dropped out. They had had a considerable amount of marching already on the 20th & carrying full marching order, told on them. The Bn arrived at WANQUENTIN at 6.30 am.	TSW
	22nd		Bn settled down for day, but orders received about 1 pm that Bn must be ready to move at short notice. Buses were to arrive about 6 pm but did not come until 9.30 pm.	
	~~23rd~~		Bn arrived at BERTANCOURT about 2.30 am & proceeded to [illegible] with extra SAA & bombs & picks & shovels. They immediately proceeded to the British front line occupied by Durhams & lined up on the tape 300 yds in front. Owing to guides not knowing some of the roads, the Bn were only just in time, the barrage coming down at 4.55 am nevertheless, the men jumped off smartly to time.	
	22nd - 28th		Report on the operations from 22nd Aug to 28 Aug is attached.	[initials] Appendix III

1875 Wt. W593/826 1,000,000 4/15 J.B.C. & A. A.D.S.S./Forms/C. 2118.

Army Form C. 2118.

Instructions regarding War Diaries and Intelligence Summaries are contained in F. S. Regs., Part II. and the Staff Manual respectively. Title pages will be prepared in manuscript.

WAR DIARY
or
INTELLIGENCE SUMMARY.
(*Erase heading not required.*)

1/4 Bn The Royal Scots Q of R

Place	Date	Hour	Summary of Events and Information	Remarks and references to Appendices
			August 1918. Page V	Rif Map
MERCATEL				
M35 & 34	28 – 31		The Bn arrived in bivouac area near MERCATEL (M35 & 34) about 8 am on the morning of 28th. From the 28th until the 31st Coys were refitted and reorganised as far as possible. Salvage work was done on the area near the camp.	FRANCE Sheet 51B SW
			On the 29th Lt Col A Maclaine Mitchell DSO resumed command of the Battn on his return from leave.	PBb
			On the 30th the B.G.C addressed all ranks of the Battn and expressed his admiration of the splendid work it had carried out.	
			On the evening of 30th warning order received from Bde that the Battn would move on the following day to position in support to 155 Bde about U14 c.	PBb
			On the 31st the Battn moved at 4.50 pm to relieve a Battn of the 167 Bde and to be in support to 155 Bde. Hqrs being established at U14 a.1.7 about 11 pm	

A6945 Wt. W11422/M1160 350,000 12/16 D. D. & L. Forms/C./2118/14.

Instructions regarding War Diaries and Intelligence Summaries are contained in F. S. Regs., Part II. and the Staff Manual respectively. Title pages will be prepared in manuscript.

WAR DIARY
or
INTELLIGENCE SUMMARY.
(Erase heading not required.)

1/4 Battn The Royal Scots Q.R.

Army Form C. 2118.

Place	Date	Hour	Summary of Events and Information	Remarks and references to Appendices
			August 1918 Page V	
			General	
			The health of the battn has been good throughout the month. The success of the first operations it has undertaken in France and the increased allotments of leave has had great effect on the spirits of all ranks	ABC
			Strength return for the month is appended	Appendix
			A Bristowe Capt. Asst Adj for Lt Col Comdg 1/4 Bn The Royal Scots Q.R.	

A6945 Wt. W11422/M1160 350,000 12/16 D. D. & L. Forms/C./2118/14.

H.Q. **Warning Order** Appendix II August

The 1st Royal Scots will relieve the 7th Royal Scots in the line on the 13th inst. No further details have so far been received from Bde but the distribution of the Bn after relief will be as follows –

D Coy. relieve No. 3 Coy. of R.S. in the Right Front
B " " " 1 " " " " Left "
A " " " 2 " " " " Right Support
C " " " 4 " " " " Left "

O.C. Coys will tomorrow reconnoitre their new lines as far as possible & may send a small proportion of platoon & section commanders to do likewise. These should however report at the H.Q. of the Coy they are relieving for permission.

A Bristowe Capt

11 Aug. 1918.

Lieut & Adjt
1/4 Royal Scots (Q.R.R.)

Appendix I
August

[illegible] (4th Royal Scots) [illegible]
[illegible] Scheme [illegible]

1. Boundaries

(a) The Southern boundary [illegible] 3 [illegible]

(b) The Northern boundary [illegible] B.27.c.7.7 – B.21.d.6.5 – B.22.a.0.0 – [illegible] 8.4. [illegible]

(c) The inter-Battn boundary [illegible] 23 [illegible] C [illegible] along [illegible]

2. Brigade Disposition

(a)
7th Sea. Rifles on Right. South of inter-Bn boundary
1st Royal Scots [illegible] North
4th Royal Scots
1 Coy. in GULLY POST
3 " " BROWN LINE

(b) Battalion Dispositions
A Coy. in GULLY POST & whole reserve [illegible] POST LINE
D, B, C Coys. respectively [illegible] BROWN LINE [illegible] defence – [illegible] held as local reserve to BROWN LINE.
Bn. Hqrs. B.27.c.7.1

(c) Coy Dispositions
D Coy. from Southern Boundary to BROWN LINE at B.27.d.35.10.
B Coy. from this point to B.27.b.4.5
C " " " " Northern Boundary

3. Copies of Brigade Defence Scheme [illegible] circulated for information

6 Aug 1918

P. Bristowe Capt.
[illegible] Adjt
4 Royal Scots (QER)

Office

Appendix II

August

1/4 Bn. The Royal Scots (Q.E.R.)
Order No. 20
by
Major J. Mowat Slater, Comdg.

Map Ref. PONT DU JOUR 1/10,000. 12 Aug. 1918.

1. On the 13 Aug. the 4th Royal Scots will relieve 7th Royal Scots in the Left Sub-Section, & on relief 7th R.S. will take over the portion of the BROWN LINE at present held by 4th R.S.

2. Coys. of this Bn. will relieve those of 7th R.S. as laid down in Warning Order issued yesterday. Coys. of 7th R.S. will take over the portions of BROWN LINE held by the relieving Coy. of 4th R.S.
Inter-Coy. Boundary runs as follows:-
B.23.c.7.5. B23.c.00.55. B.22.c.9.3. B.21.d.6.0.

3. Advance parties as under from Coys. & HQ. will leave their respective HQ. at 7 am.
1 Officer per Coy. 1 N.C.O. per platoon. Coy. Gas N.C.O. & 1 L.G. N.C.O. per Coy.
HQrs. I.O., Sig. O., a proportion of scouts & runners.
Advance parties from 7th R.S. will report early on morning of relief to take over from Coys. 4th R.S.

4. Coys. will move by sections of 50 yds. interval at the following times:-
B. Coy. at 9 am. D. Coy. at 10.30 am. C. Coy. at 12 noon. A. Coy. at 1 pm.
& will meet guides from 7th R.S. at points & times to be arranged mutually between OC. Coys. 4th & 7th R.S.

5. Defence Schemes, trench stores, maps etc, will be handed & taken over & receipts forwarded to Bn. HQ. 12 hours after completion of relief.
200 L.G. mags. per Coy. with cases & carriers complete will be handed & taken over.

6. In case of attack during relief, Coys. will man nearest trenches & report to Bn. H.Q.

7. On the night of relief, all rations will come up by railway, & Coys. will take over existing arrangements of 7th R.S. for water & rations. On subsequent nights, arrangements will probably be made for rations of D & A. Coys. to be sent up by limber.

8. Bn. HQ. will close at B.27.c.7.1 at 12.30pm. and re-open at B.21.a.8.2. at the same hour.
After relief, HQ., 7th SR. & 7th R.S. will be at B.21.c.7.1. and B.27.a.2.5. respectively.

9. Reliefs must be completed by 5 pm. completion to be reported to Bn. HQ. by code word "CRIKEY".

10. Acknowledge.

Issued at 5.15 pm

P. Bristowe Carr

Lieut. & A/adjt

1/4 Royal Scots (Q.E.R.)

Appendix 3 August

Report on operations from 22nd. Aug. to 28th. Aug. 1918.

Map Reference FRANCE Sheet 51B. S.W.

At 9-30 p.m. on the night of the 22nd. Aug. 1918, the Bn. left WANQUENTIN by bus for a debussing point on the HAMELINCOURT - AGNY Road about M.32.d. Considerable delay was experienced in getting the Bn. to this point owing to the great congestion of military traffic throughout the road. S.A.A. and bombs, flares and tools were issued on the roadside. Companies were to march to a Brigade point of assembly at M.33.d. Owing to thevvery late arrival of "C" and "D" Coys. it was decided not to issue them extra ammunition etc. Great difficulty was experienced in getting the Bn. to the point of assembly on account of the congestion of the roads and tracks.

The Battalion moved off about 3-15 a.m. with guides furnished by the Durham Light Infantry. The Bn. was to be sheltered in front line trenches about S.5.b.&.d. and S.6.c. On the way over, Bn. was mislead by the guides in charge and there was a halt of 5 minutes in order to allow the guides the opportunity of regaining their direction.

At this time the enemy sent over several gas shells and masks had to be worn. The guide reported having found the track which should take us forward to the front line system in front of which a tape had been laid to mark our line of deployment.

As it was now 4-35 a.m., "A" Coy. moved Southwards along the tape, "B" and "C" Coys. moving inrear and in the same direction. They had barely got to their correct positions on the tape when the time came for them to advance. At this time "D" Coy. was unable to get to the tape and was therefore ordered to get into a front line trench.

ZERO hour for the attack was 4-55 a.m.

The artillery barrage came down at 4-55 a.m. on line approximately 300 yds. East of the line of deployment. The barrage remained on its opening barrage line for 12 minutes and then lifted by bounds of 200 yds to and beyond final objectives.

The 7th. Royal Scots were on the left of the Battalion and the London Scottish on the right. The rate of advance was 100 yds. per 4 minutes in order to conform with the London Scottish.

"A" Coy. had for its objective SPINNEY AVENUE from its junction with LONG ALLEY Southwards to the River COJEUL; "B" Coy. to the sunk road between the same two points, and "C" Coy. the Sump trench between same two points.

Coys. gained their objectives without great opposition taking 100 prisoners and 15 Machine Guns besides other booty.

The second Coy. wave passed through the final objective and exploited our own front in conjunction with the tanks for a distance of 400 yards. We had one section of tanks; the right tank was given a strong point marked CRUCIFIX as its objective in S.6.d.5.1., the left tank a strong point about the junction of LONG ALLEY and SPINNEY AVENUE. The third tank traversed the wire and was available to go to the assistance of the infantry. A Bn. scout was given to each tank to act as liaison between the tanks and the infantry.

The Bn. was arranged in depth, lines being thinly held, defensive scheme being in depth. Consolidation was immediately undertaken. "D" Coy. was ordered to occupy a position in N.33.c.6.5. in order to keep touch with the 7th. Royal Scots on our left. To conform with the Bn. on our right (London Scottish) an outpost line was thrown forward to BOIRY Reserve Trench.

On the night of the 24th. "D" Coy. was sent forward to fill a gap between the 156th. and 157th. Inf. Bdes. This they did by establishing 4 strong points covering a distance of 1200 yards. This area was severely shelled with gas shells and being low lying there was heavy gas concentration necessitating the Coy. wearing their masks

/masks for the greater part of the night. On the morning of the 26th. this Coy. was withdrawn to MARTIN Trench.

On the afternoon of the 26th., orders were recieved to concentrate Bn. East of SPINNEY AVENUE. The Bn. less "D" Coy. were sheltered in BOIRBY Reserve Trench and MARTIN Trench, "D" Coy. concentrating on road junction at N.33.c.

Provisional orders were given to occupy HINDENBURG LINE, 2 Coys. to be placed North of the River and 2 Coys. South of the river. This was not done however, but a concentration of the Bn. was ordered on the road junction already referred to.

Verbal orders were received for a night advance from CROW Trench in a South Easterly direction to FONTAINE WOOD and LEMON BRIDGE. The orders for this advance were cancelled. "D" Coy. were sent to occupy a portion of CROW Trench from the road in N.35.a. to the 7th. Royal Scots; "B" Coy. were sheltered in some suitable ground 200 yards in rear; "C" and "A" Coys. together with Bn.Hqrs. were kept on the roadside in N.33.b. for the night.

At 9 a.m. on the 27th. orders were received for the Brigade to attack at 10 a.m. with the Canadians on our left and the 157th. Inf. Bde. on our right. ZERO hour was 10 a.m. A barrage was arranged for at the rate of 100 yds. per 4 minutes. The right of the Bn. was to be directed on U.2.central. "D" "A" and "C" Coys. advanced in waves and followed the barrage and pushed right forward to their objectives reaching same about 2 p.m. "B" Coy. were held in reserve. A further advance from this point was impossible as the Canadians on our left were held up by serious Machine Gun fire on their flank. The left was the directing flank.

An outpost line was formed round FONTAINE CROISILLES in touch with the 7th. Royal Scots and Canadians on our left and endeavours were made to get in touch with the 157th. Inf. Bde. As the 157th. Bde. did not get as far forward as expected, it was not until 1 a.m. that touch was ultimately got with them at a point in the HINDENBURG System.

Late at night orders were recieved that the 57th. Division might relieve us during the night. This order was amended by substitution of the 2nd. Canadians who made themselves responsible for the whole of our front. Ultimately a Bn. of the Loyal North Lancashire Regt. arrived to take over the line, but in the interval we had been ordered to withdraw. The Bn. withdraw and assembled in ROTTEN Trench and moved to a bivouac area in the neighbourhood of MERCATEL.

Throughout the attack 340 prisoners were taken and 35 M.G's. Our casualties for the whole of the operations were 5 Officers and 240 Other Ranks.

J. Mowat Malcolm
Major.
for ~~Major~~ Comdg. 1/4th Bn.
The Royal Scots

30th. August, 1918.

War Diary August 1918

Additions to Strength

	off	or
From Hospital	-	53
Reinforcements	4	4
	4	57

Deductions from Strength

	off	or
To Hospl Sick + NYD	-	88
now in Hospl over 7 days	-	20
Transf. to Gordon Highrs	-	1
Reposted to 2nd R Scots	-	1
Sigs att T.M Battys now struck off	-	2
To 10th Liverpool Regt + struck off	1	-
Classd. B.2 "	1	-
Invalided to UK	1	-
To UK as Candidate for Comn	-	1
Battle Casualties:-		
Killed	.	23
Wounded	4	116
Died of Wounds	-	1
Wounded + missing	-	4
Missing	-	16
	7	273

Strength of Bn 31/8/18

	off	or
With Battn	19	426
Transport	1	55
Bde Transport	-	1
" Hdqrs Runners + Scouts	-	4
at Courses of Instruction	4	12
at 1st Army Rest Camp	1	5
Leave to UK	5	103
Detached	4	43
Duty with Wounded Offrs Kit	-	3
Guards at [illegible]		6
Salvage Party	1	14
Ammunition Unloading Party	-	14
In Hospital (under 7 days) ORs	7	91
	42	777

Attached:-

	off	or
M.O	1	-
R.C Chaplain	1	-
P.T + B.F Instr.	-	1
A O C (armourer Sgt)	-	1
	2	2

Sept 1918 -
Royal Scots Fusiliers

Vol. 6

War Diary

1/4th Bn Royal Scots Fusiliers

155th Infantry Brigade

52nd Division

VOL. V.

Sept. 1918

13. B.
15 sheets

Instructions regarding War Diaries and Intelligence Summaries are contained in F. S. Regs., Part II. and the Staff Manual respectively. Title pages will be prepared in manuscript.

WAR DIARY ~~or INTELLIGENCE SUMMARY.~~ of 4th Bn Royal Scots Fus. for September 1918

(Erase heading not required.)

Army Form C. 2118.

Place	Date	Hour	Summary of Events and Information	Remarks and references to Appendices
	1918			
BULLECOURT	1 Sept.		'C' Coy sent out a Patrol with one light T.M.B. which was caught by M.G. fire in JOY RIDE trench, several killed and wounded and L.T.M. temporarily lost. More casualties in MARE LANE from Snipers, enfilading M.G. fire, and shell fire. "A" Coy sent out a similar patrol in front of the FACTORY towards BUNNY HUG trench. This patrol drove 2 M.G. Posts out into the open with bombs and rifle grenades, and inflicted casualties on the enemy with rifle and L.G. fire. Lieut. G. CLARK (patrol commdr.) then sent back for a L.T.M. and drove some more posts out into the open inflicting casualties on them.	
			Orders received from Brigade at 5.55 p.m. to attack. "A" Coy under Capt. W.F. TEMPLETON on left and "C" Coy under Capt. J.H. JOHNSTONE on right, each with 3 platoons in first wave and 1 platoon in second wave. Mopping up was done by "D" Coy in three parties under Lieut. W.L. HODGSON. "B" Coy under Capt. W.A. MUIR were kept in Reserve. Orders for this attack were given to Coy Commdrs verbally at Bn. Conference. Barrage stood 10 minutes and then moved 100 yards every	

(A9175) Wt W2353/P560 600,000 12/17 D. D. & L. Sch. 52a. Forms/C2118/15.

Instructions regarding War Diaries and Intelligence Summaries are contained in F. S. Regs., Part II. and the Staff Manual respectively. Title pages will be prepared in manuscript.

WAR DIARY of 4th Bn. Royal Scots Fus. for September 1918
~~INTELLIGENCE SUMMARY.~~
(Erase heading not required.)

Army Form C. 2118.

2

Place	Date	Hour	Summary of Events and Information	Remarks and references to Appendices
	1918			
BULLECOURT	1 Spt.	-	4 minutes. The Bn. got well away under the barrage and found the enemy barrage very weak. Ground was found very much cut up from last year, and very favourable to an advance against M.G. fire. 2/Lieut J.B. FREW of "C" Coy saw a party of enemy in TANK TRENCH to his right, firing on 4th K.O.S.B. He started bombing down the trench sending Sergt. BURNETT with 2 men round the rear of the trench into it below the enemy to bomb up the trench. Sergt. BURNETT and Pte STEVENSON bombed up this trench covered by the rifle fire of Pte McCALLUM who fired standing on the parados. Fifty two prisoners and 4 M.Gs surrendered to this platoon. "A" Coy reached its objectives with "C" Coy close to them. 4th K.O.S.B. were counter attacked in TANK TRENCH. "C" Coy then dropped a flank back and so did "B" Coy. The Reserve were then ordered up to fill the gap between "C" Coy and 4th K.O.S.B. Owing to the darkness of the night many runners lost their way. 2 Officers and 76 OR prisoners passed through our Hdqs. 2/Lieut VINE was wounded in leg in forenoon, Lieut W.L HODGSON was also wounded	

(A9175) Wt W2358/P560 600,000 12/17 D. D. & L. Sch. 52a. Forms/C2118/15.

Cl.

Instructions regarding War Diaries and Intelligence Summaries are contained in F. S. Regs., Part II. and the Staff Manual respectively. Title pages will be prepared in manuscript.

3

WAR DIARY of 4th Bn. Royal Scots Fus. for September 1918
~~INTELLIGENCE SUMMARY.~~
(Erase heading not required.)

Army Form C. 2118.

Place	Date	Hour	Summary of Events and Information	Remarks and references to Appendices
BULLECOURT	1918 1st Sept		in the hand at night, the command of "D" Coy passing to Lieut D. FRASER, Lieut G. CLARK and 2/Lieut W. GUNN were also wounded the same evening. Difficulty was experienced with rations and water owing to darkness, wire and narrow C.Ts.	
	2nd		Troops on our LEFT attacked again during the morning the 156th Inf. Brigade passing through us. Some of our barrage fell short and landed around the trenches occupied by "A" Coy. Considerable progress was made by 7 a.m. and "D" Coy followed by "B" Coy under some hostile shell and M.G. fire moved into the HINDENBURG LINE W of QUEANT and bombed down towards the HIRONDELLE RIVER. "D" Coy having cleared front and support lines for 250 yards took up their position facing E. "B" Coy then went through them and did the same. Both Coys met with some opposition B Coy having one man killed and ~~2~~ Lieut W. McLELLAN wounded and 6 ORs. L.T.M. found very useful. Pte HENDERSON of "B" Coy again did good work	

Ch.

(A9175) Wt W2358/P360 600,000 12/17 D. D. & L. Sch. 52a. Forms/C2118/15.

Instructions regarding War Diaries and Intelligence Summaries are contained in F. S. Regs., Part II. and the Staff Manual respectively. Title pages will be prepared in manuscript.

4

WAR DIARY ~~or INTELLIGENCE SUMMARY.~~ of 4th Bn. Royal Scots Fus. for Sept. 1918

(Erase heading not required.)

Army Form C. 2118.

Place	Date 1918	Hour	Summary of Events and Information	Remarks and references to Appendices
QUEANT	2nd Sept.		"A" Coy in Support in HINDENBURG LINE, "C" Coy in Support in valley to N. "D" Coy and "B" Coy patrols towards QUEANT found all quiet. Captain C.E. HAMILTON M.O. (U.S.A) suffering from malaria was found being carried forward on a stretcher to new Bn. Hdqs. and was sent back to A.D.S.	
	3rd Sept.		Bn. Hdqs. moved to "A" Coy. Hdqs at 5am. Bn. attacked down HINDENBURG LINE at 5.30 am, order of attack B, D, A, C Coys, no opposition. 2 ALSATIAN prisoners stated their Regt. retired at 10pm the night before. About 50 prisoners passed advanced Bn. Hdqs. they having waited behind in dug-outs. "B" Coy captured 5 77 mm guns and 3 10.5 cm guns also many T.Ms and M.Gs taken but no time them; five heavy and 2 light M.Gs sent in from forward area. 2 8.2 cm guns also found in our area but already claimed by 2nd Scots Guards.	
			154th Inf. Brigade came through QUEANT in the morning. We relieved them in the HINDENBURG LINE in the afternoon taking	

Ck.

(A9475) Wt W2358/P360 600,000 12/17 D. D. & L. Sch. 52a. Forms/C2118/15

Instructions regarding War Diaries and Intelligence Summaries are contained in F. S. Regs., Part II. and the Staff Manual respectively. Title pages will be prepared in manuscript.

5

WAR DIARY ~~or INTELLIGENCE SUMMARY~~. of 4th Bn. Royal Scots Fus. for Sept. 1918

(Erase heading not required.)

Army Form C. 2118.

Place	Date	Hour	Summary of Events and Information	Remarks and references to Appendices
QUEANT	Sept 1918 3		over Line from S.W. of QUEANT to S.E of PRONVILLE. B. Coy on Right "A" Coy centre, "D" Coy Left, "C" Coy in Reserve. Bn. prepared to face N. by E or S.	
	4th		Bn. rested and commenced reorganizing in above Line	
	5th } 6th }		Reorganization carried on and a commencement made with further Lewis Gun training. Orders received from Brigade	
	7th		that Bn. would march to area near ST LEGER and to be clear of the HINDENBURG LINE by 5 am on the 7th.	
ST LEGER	7th		Bn. marched off at 05.00 via LAGNICOURT, NOREUIL and ECOUST to bivouac area S.E. of ST LEGER arriving about 8.30 am. Accomodation consisting of some old dug-outs and bivouac shelters	
	8th		Bn. Church parade held in Camp area.	
	9th/10th		Reorganizing and training carried out the latter interfered with by rain	
	11th		Training carried out. Divisional Concert in afternoon.	

(A9175) Wt W2352/P360 600,000 12/17 D. D. & L. Sch. 52a. Forms/C2118/15

Cl.

Instructions regarding War Diaries and Intelligence Summaries are contained in F. S. Regs., Part II. and the Staff Manual respectively. Title pages will be prepared in manuscript.

6

WAR DIARY ~~or INTELLIGENCE SUMMARY.~~ of 4th Bn. Royal Scots Fus. for Sept. 1918

(Erase heading not required.)

Army Form C. 2118.

Place	Date	Hour	Summary of Events and Information	Remarks and references to Appendices
Nr. ST LEGER	1918 Sept. 12/13th		Training carried on, Bn. bathed and clean clothing issued	
	14th		Brigade Route march at 4.30 am to Tank Demonstration at 1st Tank Corps Hdqs. BOISLEUX ST MARC.	
			Warning order received from Brigade that Bn. would move into Line on night of 15th inst. C.O. reconnoitred Sector to be taken over.	
	15th		Bn marched out of Bivouac Area at 2.30 p.m. and halted in HIRONDELLE VALLEY just W of QUEANT about 5 p.m. evening meal being served there. Move into HINDENBURG LINE commenced about 6.30 p.m. and relief completed 11.30 p.m. Dispositions – B Coy counter attack Coy for 4th K.O.S.B. D Coy and A Coy main line of resistance. C Coy in reserve to Bn behind Bn HQ. –	
MOEUVRES SECTOR.	16th		Day passed without incident of note. CO visited line and worked out Scheme of Defence for main line of resistance. – Coy Commanders Conference. – Enemy shelled area with 77mm and 4.2 and 5.9 HE. – 5 killed and 5 wounded on ration carrying parties to K.O.S.B.	
	17th		Enemy sent over Mustard Gas at Stand to C Coy area receiving particular attention All day enemy shelled support sector with 77 mm. 5.9 and 4.2 H.E. mixed with Gas	

C.G.

Instructions regarding War Diaries and Intelligence Summaries are contained in F. S. Regs., Part II. and the Staff Manual respectively. Title pages will be prepared in manuscript.

WAR DIARY
or
~~INTELLIGENCE SUMMARY.~~
(Erase heading not required.)

1/4 R S F.
September 1918

Army Form C. 2118.

Place	Date	Hour	Summary of Events and Information	Remarks and references to Appendices
MOEUVRES SECTOR.	17th		Gas and mustard Gas - 1910. S.O.S sent up from front line. The enemy barrage fell on HINDENBURG FRONT and support lines - Enemy advance directed by planes dropping flares. Our barrage came down about 1915 and situation very vague all wires being cut. Message came from C.O from KOSB Hqrs to stand to. - All coys notified and Bn Hqrs organised - Enemy succeeded in entering and obtaining possession of MOEUVRES KOSB. centre and left Coys being driven back. Our B. Coy ordered to go forward and take up a position in SWAN LANE gaining touch with KOSB. - Battle stations manned. 2200 all was evidently quiet except for occasional bursts of enemy MG fire.. KOSB. right and right centre coys intact in touch with Guards on Right where enemy attacks were met with the bayonet and frustrated. 1 Coy 5th R.S.F. arrived from Reserve and sent up to find touch with D Coy K.O.S.B. and fill gap between D Coy K.O.S.B. and 5th HLI on left holding bank just on edge of MOEUVRES S.W. corner - Enemy attack held up and a defensive line established. C & B Coys KOSB combining and forming left Coy in HINDENBURG LINE astride CEMETERY SUPPORT.	

(A9175) Wt. W2358/P569 600,000 12/17 D. D. & L. Sch. 52a. Forms/C2118/15.

Instructions regarding War Diaries and Intelligence Summaries are contained in F. S. Regs., Part II. and the Staff Manual respectively. Title pages will be prepared in manuscript.

WAR DIARY
or
~~INTELLIGENCE SUMMARY.~~
(Erase heading not required.)

8 Septr 1918. 8.

Army Form C. 2118.

Place	Date	Hour	Summary of Events and Information	Remarks and references to Appendices
The field	17th.		situation still obscure. Night passed without further incident.	
			Casualties from this attack were 5 OR killed [illegible] wounded.	
	18.		The enemy shelled the area West of MOEUVRES intermittently during the day.	
			At 5.30 pm S.O.S. flare was put up by line battalion, our B Coy. Germans	
			entered HINDENBURG SUPPORT LINE at junction with SWAN LANE E20 a 20.99 and	
			succeeded in gaining a footing in both trenches. He got almost to junction	
			of HINDENBURG SUPPORT LINE and SHORT STREET. 2nd Lt. D. M. YUILLE and 3 men	
			bombed enemy back to E14 C 05 were 2/Lt YUILLE was wounded. Party	
			withdrew. Later trench was finally cleared of enemy to E14 C 15.	
			Remainder of night passed without incident. Casualties 1 off. [illegible] wounded 2 OR killed 6 wounded	
			Enemy dropped some Mustard Gas Shells on our Support Area during the	
			night and Capt Johnstone & 2nd Lts Rankine & Alexander went to hospital	
			Gassed as a result. The following OR were also gassed by the	
			Gas shell bombardment: A Coy 8 B Coy 4 C Coy 23	
	19.		During the day our heavies kept up fire on Eastern part of	
			MOEUVRES and Canal. At 7 pm our barrage opened on MOEUVRES	

CB.

(A9175) Wt W2358/P360 600,000 12/17 D. D. & L. Sch. 52a. Forms/C2118/15.

Instructions regarding War Diaries and Intelligence Summaries are contained in F. S. Regs., Part II. and the Staff Manual respectively. Title pages will be prepared in manuscript.

Army Form C. 2118.

WAR DIARY
or
~~INTELLIGENCE SUMMARY~~.
(Erase heading not required.)

9 Septr 1918.

Place	Date	Hour	Summary of Events and Information	Remarks and references to Appendices
The field	19		It remained stationary for 5 minutes & then moved forward 100 yards per four minutes, finally resting on the canal. Our A.B & D. coys together with two Coys 7th HLI and 2 Coys 5th R.S.F. attacked the village at 7 am. Our northern boundary was line due East & West through RED HOUSE E14 c 8 7 to trench running East & West from E20 a 2 9 to Canal. All objectives were taken. Posts were established at E14 d 2 5, E14 d 2 6 (where touch was obtained with 7th HLI and at E14 d 5 5. Our right Coy went too far south & got touch with 5 R S.F. at E20 b 11, but failed to get touch on left. C Coy the mopping up party cleared the village & established post at E20 b 19. The line between this post & our A Coy at E20 b 11. was so thinly held that 1 coy 4 KOSB were brought in to fill the gap during the night & the morning of 20th. Casualties. 4 Lts KEAN & INGLIS wounded. OR. 16 wounded 4 [illegible]	
	20.		The positions gained by us last night were maintained. The enemy shelled MOEUVRES with HE & gas shells. The battalion was relieved on night of 20/21 Septr by 4th Bn Royal Scots and went to D16. battalion headquarters being at D16 b 40. On the way back the enemy shelled	

(A9175) Wt W2358/P360 600,000 12/17 D. D. & L. Sch. 52a. Forms/C2118/15.

Cls

Instructions regarding War Diaries and Intelligence Summaries are contained in F. S. Regs., Part II. and the Staff Manual respectively. Title pages will be prepared in manuscript.

WAR DIARY
or
~~INTELLIGENCE SUMMARY.~~
(*Erase heading not required.*)

10/ Septr 1918.

Army Form C. 2118.

Place	Date	Hour	Summary of Events and Information	Remarks and references to Appendices
Thefild.	20		our support areas with Mustard Gas Shells. 2/Lt A.N. Harvey went to hospital	
			as result. 3 OR were also gassed. Our casualties during 20th were.	
			2/Lt A.N. HARVEY gassed 2/Lt E. KNIGHT Killed. O.R. 4 Killed [illegible] wounded to hospital [illegible]	
	21		Battalion rested and reorganisation was commenced. A & C.	
	~~22~~		Coys were carrying party to 4th Royal Scots and these Coys suffered	
			casualties by enemy bombardment of front and support areas.	
	22		Battalion rested and completed reorganisation. D Coy was ordered to	
			relieve C Coy of 5th R.S.F. ~~at~~ just West of TADPOLE COPSE. C & A Coys	
			carried rations &c to 4 Royal Scots. When our D Coy relieved C Coy	
			5 R.S.F. they came under the orders of O.C. 5 R.S.F.	
	23		Battalion commenced salvage operations in D16. Battalion	
			received order stating it would be under orders of 156 Bde. Later	
			Battalion received orders to relieve 4th R Royal Scots taking over	
			sector ~~from~~ East & west from E14 central (inclusive) to trench running	
			from E20a 98 East to Canal. Order of Coys from N to South was	
			D, C & A Coys C Coy had 2 platoons of B Coy holding posts. The remainder	

(A9175) Wt W2355/P360 600,000 12/17 D. D. & L. Sch. 52a. Forms/C2118/15.

C.S.

Instructions regarding War Diaries and Intelligence Summaries are contained in F. S. Regs., Part II. and the Staff Manual respectively. Title pages will be prepared in manuscript.

11.

WAR DIARY
or
INTELLIGENCE SUMMARY.
(Erase heading not required.)

Army Form C. 2118.

Place	Date	Hour	Summary of Events and Information	Remarks and references to Appendices
The field.	23		of B Coy was at B Coy Hdqrs at E 13 d 95. Bn Hq was at E 13 b 31. Relief was completed at midnight on ~~evening~~ of ~~24th~~ 23rd Septr. 2/Lt MOFFAT reported for duty 23rd was posted to B Coy. OR 3 wounded 2 gassed 5 to hospital sick	
	24.		During the day both artilleries were active. A small percentage of gas was reported in MOEUVRES. A party of 40 OR & 1 officer carried Battalion rations from dump to Coy Hdqrs at night. Casualties for day OR 1 wounded 2 to hospital sick	
	25.		At 4.50 am Enemy T.M. barrage was opened on E 14 central and on Village. At same time a party of the enemy attacked E 14 central and forced the post there to withdraw. Our SOS flare went up and our barrage came down on enemy positions near canal & further east. Enemy did not hold post. We re-established post at 7.50 am. 2/Lt A. KNIGHT was wounded. Other casualties were 2/LT W. KIDDET to hospital gassed, OR. 11 gassed 3 OR killed 5 OR wounded sick to hospital 3. No other incident of importance occurred during the day.	
	26		At 5 am a party of the enemy estimated at 50 to 60 attacked E 14 central	

(A9175) Wt W2355/P360 600,000 12/17 D. D. & L. **Sch. 52a.** Forms/C2118/15.

C.G.

Instructions regarding War Diaries and Intelligence Summaries are contained in F. S. Regs., Part II. and the Staff Manual respectively. Title pages will be prepared in manuscript.

12

WAR DIARY
or
~~INTELLIGENCE SUMMARY.~~
(Erase heading not required.)

Sept 1918.

Army Form C. 2118.

Place	Date	Hour	Summary of Events and Information	Remarks and references to Appendices
The field	26		and forced our post there to withdraw. Enemy occupied post and pushed on towards the village. Our post took up a position ~~from~~ E14 c87 to Red House E14 c96. At 9.30 a.m. two of our parties, one from E13 d87 and the other from RED HOUSE E14 c96 commenced working towards the post with a view to forcing enemy to vacate post at E14 central. At the same time our Stokes Guns opened fire on ditch running NE from E14 central to Canal. Enemy withdrew in small numbers & at 10.45 am we reoccupied post at E14 central. At 11am Lt Col. Cruddas commanding our Battalion handed over command of the Battalion to Major [illegible] Bruce. Lt Col. Cruddas was given command of 1st Bn. Northumberland Fusiliers. A short time after we reoccupied E14 central a party of Canadians (1 NCO + 6 men) formed a joint post with us there. During the day it was noted that the enemy guns were much quieter than usual. In the afternoon C + D + Bn. Hqrs moved to A + B Coy Hdqrs at E13 d96 Casualties for day 4 OR Killed [illegible] wounded	
	Z			

C. [illegible]

Instructions regarding War Diaries and Intelligence Summaries are contained in F. S. Regs., Part II. and the Staff Manual respectively. Title pages will be prepared in manuscript.

B

WAR DIARY
or
INTELLIGENCE SUMMARY.
(Erase heading not required.)

Army Form C. 2118.

Place	Date	Hour	Summary of Events and Information	Remarks and references to Appendices
The field.		27.	At 5.20 am an attack on a large scale was commenced. The 63rd Division passed through our area at that time. At 10 am battalion moved to P24d & bivouaced there. At 3pm battalion returned to trenches in E13b+d. Battalion was then with remainder of Brigade in Divisional reserve. Division was ordered to be prepared to defend Canal du Nord line in case of enemy Counterattack.	
		28.	Battalion still remained in ~~E~~E13b+d. Draft of 69 OR reported for duty.	
		29.	The Commanding Officer inspected draft of 69 ~~OR~~ & held Battalion parade ~~at~~ 9.15 am. when he expressed the thanks of Lt. Col. Cruddas to all ranks for the good work done by the battalion while Lt. Col. Cruddas was in Command. The Commanding Officer also informed all ranks of the important work it had performed in the MOEUVRES sector in holding all positions and thus enabling attack of 27th to materialise. At 10 am the Commanding Officer with O.C. Coys & 3 other officers reconnoitred	

Ch.

(A9175) Wt W2358/P360 600,000 12/17 D. D. & L. Sch. 52a. Forms/C2118/15.

Instructions regarding War Diaries and Intelligence Summaries are contained in F. S. Regs., Part II. and the Staff Manual respectively. Title pages will be prepared in manuscript.

Army Form C. 2118.

WAR DIARY
or
~~INTELLIGENCE SUMMARY.~~

(Erase heading not required.)

14 Septr 1918

Place	Date	Hour	Summary of Events and Information	Remarks and references to Appendices
The field	29		the area from Moeuvres to ANNEUX, FONTAINE-NOTRE-DAME, CANTAING, and GRAINCOURT. Battalion was engaged on salvage work. At 9 pm battalion received warning order to be prepared to move to ANNEUX–GRAINCOURT area at 9 tomorrow. Sick to hospital 6 O.R.	
	30.		Battalion left area at E13 b+d at 9 am + moved by march route to ANNEUX where it was billetted in cellars in the village. At 2 pm all officers were taken round our battle position East of ANNEUX and had the tactical situation explained to them. Coy & Bn areas were allotted + a scheme of defence discussed. At 3 pm a warning order stating that Battalion must be prepared to move to F26 b+d was received. ~~At 4.30 pm~~ At 4.30 pm battalion left ANNEUX ~~at~~ and marched to F26, where it took up position in the eastern trench of the MARQUION LINE. Bn Hqrs was at F26 d 6.9.	

[signature illegible]
[illegible] Comdg [illegible]

(A9175) Wt W2358/P360 600,000 12/17 D. D. & L. Sch. 52a. Forms/C2118/15.

Confidential

Original

7

WAR DIARY

for

October 1918

Vol XLI

1/4 Bn Royal Scots (QEK)

(1)

WAR DIARY
or
INTELLIGENCE SUMMARY.
(Erase heading not required.)

Page 1

Army Form C. 2118.

Instructions regarding War Diaries and Intelligence Summaries are contained in F. S. Regs., Part II. and the Staff Manual respectively. Title pages will be prepared in manuscript.

1/4th Bn The Royal Scots. October 1918 Volume XLI

Place	Date	Hour	Summary of Events and Information	Remarks and references to Appendices
Sh. Map France 57C NE	1/10/18		Orders received that Battalion would move to rest area in L3a	
CANAL DU NORD			the 156th Inf Bde being in Reserve to the 52nd Division & this Bn being	1/50
beside MOEUVRES.			in Reserve to this Brigade. The Bn moved off at 1700 the position	
			was a system of trenches W of CANTAING (Bn Orders No. 28 App. 1	app 1
	2nd–5th		Bn employed in salvage work & burying of dead horses.	
	6th		Intimation received at 0300 that Battalion along with the rest of Bde	
			were moving West of the CANAL DU NORD to a new bivouac area in J2,3+4	1/50 app 2
			near LOUVERVAL.	
			The march started at 0900.	
	7th		Orders received that Battalion would entrain at VAULXVRAUCOURT for	
			conveyance to TINGUES (orders app 3) On arrival at TINGUES Bn moved	app 3
IZEL	8–11		to Billets in IZEL LEZ HAMEAUX arriving there about 2000	
LEZ HAMEAUX			For the first four days Bn rested. Bathing, reorganising	
			& generally smartening itself up.	
	12		A start made with training. Tactical schemes in co-operation	
			with LTMs. Specialist work etc.	

A6945 Wt. W11422/M1160 350,000 12/16 D. D. & L. Forms/C./2118/14.

Instructions regarding War Diaries and Intelligence Summaries are contained in F. S. Regs., Part II. and the Staff Manual respectively. Title pages will be prepared in manuscript.

WAR DIARY
or
INTELLIGENCE SUMMARY.
(Erase heading not required.)

Army Form C. 2118.

Page 2. October 1918

Place	Date	Hour	Summary of Events and Information	Remarks and references to Appendices
			1/12th Bn The Royal Scots. Volume XLI	
IZEL LEZ HAMEAU.			Training in Tactical exercises was continued up to the 18th. All training was completed by 1300 after which organised sport was indulged in. A Football league was inaugurated & the best Coy team taking part in games against the other Bns & Bde HQ. "B" Coy represented the unit & carried all before it.	TBW
Ref LENS 1/100000	19/10/18		Orders issued for a march to CHATEAU de la HAIE. The Bde started at 0900 this Bn leading & marched via TILLOY LES HERMAVILLE, AUBIGNY AGNIÈRES CAMBLAIN L'ABBÉ to CHATEAU de la HAIE where it was billeted in Huts for the night.	APP IV
[illegible]	20/10/18		The Bde proceeded on its march at 0900 eastwards passing through SOUCHEZ - GIVENCHY - AVION - MARICOURT SALAUMINES to BILLY MONTIGNY where it stayed the night. The last named village was in a delapidated condition striking evidence being shown of the HUNS despicable acts of destruction.	TBW
	21/10/18		The Bde continued its march passing through HENIN LIETARD COURCELLES	TBW
AUBY	22/10/18		to AUBY where it billeted & the 22nd was spent in resting & cleaning up generally. It was noticeable that although a lot of wanton damage had been done the Huns had left in a great hurry.	TBW

A6945 Wt. W11422/M1160 350,000 12/16 D. D. & L. Forms/C./2118/14.

Instructions regarding War Diaries and Intelligence Summaries are contained in F. S. Regs., Part II. and the Staff Manual respectively. Title pages will be prepared in manuscript.

WAR DIARY
or
INTELLIGENCE SUMMARY.
(Erase heading not required.)

Army Form C. 2118.

Page 3. October 1918.

1/4th Bn The Royal Scots. VOLUME XLI

Place	Date	Hour	Summary of Events and Information	Remarks and references to Appendices
AUBY.	24/10/18		The Bde continued to march Eastwards to the COUTICHES & MOLINEL area the march was through the villages of ROOST WARENDIN - WARENDIN - LAPLACETTE FLINES - ORCHIES ROAD - COUTICHES, thus Bn marched on to MOLINEL where it was billetted.	App V TOW
	25/10/18 - 26/10/18		The Bn was engaged in road repairing & also did some training.	TOW
	27/10/18		The Bde again moved Eastwards preparatory to taking over the line held at present by the 12th Divisions. The march was through ORCHIES - BEUVRY - LES - ORCHIES - RUE du ROSIER to LECELLES where it was billetted for the night	TOW
	28/10/18		Orders received that this Bn would take over the left support from the 9th Bn Royal Fusiliers (36th Inf Bde, 12th Division) Bn marched to ~~[illegible]~~ Rue de CHORETTE where guides took companies to their different posts Bn HQ being billetted at FRESNOY.	APP. VI TOW
	29/10/18 - 31/10/18		Battalion were put under six hours notice that in event of Enemy retiring, to be prepared to pursue him.	TOW

A6945 Wt. W11422/M1160 350,000 12/16 D. D. & L. Forms/C./2118/14.

Instructions regarding War Diaries and Intelligence Summaries are contained in F. S. Regs., Part II. and the Staff Manual respectively. Title pages will be prepared in manuscript.

Army Form C. 2118.

WAR DIARY
or
INTELLIGENCE SUMMARY.
(Erase heading not required.)

Page 4 October.

Place	Date	Hour	Summary of Events and Information	Remarks and references to Appendices
			1/4 Bn The Royal Scots Volume XLI	
			General Information	
			The Battalion enjoyed a good rest & put in some helpful training.	
			The health of the troops during the latter part of the month was not very satisfactory due to influenza. This told in proportion heaviest on Officers. By the end of the month the health of the men had improved.	TSW
			Leave was continued & by the end of the month men over 9 months had all had their leave.	
			The usual strength return is appended	TSW
			T. Drummond Wilson Capt & Adjt. 1/4 Bn The Royal Scots.	

A6945 Wt. W11422/M1160 350,000 12/16 D. D. & L. Forms/C./2118/14.

War Diary October 1918

1/4 Bn. The Royal Scots

Additions to Strength

	Off	OR
Reinforcements	11	75
From Hospital	2	104
Cross-posted from 7 R Scots	-	1
	13	180

Deductions from Strength

	Off	OR
Now in Hospl over 7 days	-	25
To Hospital	-	41
Transferred to England (sick)	1	-
To Home Establishment U.K. as candidate for Comm.	-	1
	-	1
Battle Casualties:—		
Died of Wounds	-	4
Wounded	-	3
Killed	-	1
Reclassd. at I.B. Depot Calais		3
Posted to Bde T.M. Batty.	1	8
	2	87

Strength of Battalion at 31/10/18

	Off	OR
With Battalion	20	450
Leave to UK	4	143
Courses of Instruction	1	28
Rest Camp	-	4
Detached	1	37
In Hospital (OR under 7 days)	10	28
Reinforcements at Divl Recn Camp	-	5
	36	695

Attached

	Off	OR
M.O. Officer	1	-
from 7 R Scots	3	
P.T. Instructor	-	1
A.O.C. armr/sgt.	-	1
	4	2

SECRET. 1/4th.Bn. The Royal Scots (Q.R.R.)

War Diary
App. I

Bn. ORDER No.28
by
Lieut-Colonel A. Maclaine Mitchell, DS.O., Comdg.

- -

Ref. map FRANCE 57C.N.E. 1/20,000. 1st. October, 1918.

1. (a) The 62nd. Divn. is relieving the 63rd.Divn. in the line on the night of 1/2nd.Oct.1918.
   (b) The 155th.Bde. will be Divl.reserve in L.3.a.&.c.

2. The 4th. Royal Scots will march to L.2.a.&.c. in the following order:-
   A;B;C;D; and HQ.Coys.
   Coys. will be divided into two with 100 yds. distance between half companies and 100 yds. between Coys.
   "A" Coy. will pass the starting point at E.28.a.2.0. cross roads at 1700 and will be followed at 100 yds. distance by "B" Coy., likewise "C" and "D" Coys. Route to be followed will be through GRAINCOURT to cross roads at L.1.a.9.6.

3. In the event of hostile aircraft approaching, the Bn. will halt and take as much cover as possible at the side of the road. Men must not look up at the plane.

4. Transport will follow in rear of the Bn. and will be brigaded at a spot to be selected by the B.T.O. Cookers will be sent up to the Bn. if a concealed position can be found.

5. Men will carry their greatcoats in their packs.

6. Rations for consumption tomorrow will be carried.

7. Actual position which Coys. will occupy will be pointed out to them on arrival at the new area.

8. Administrative H.Q. will stay with the Transport.

9. Officers valises, Coy. stores, tents and shelters will be dumped at E.27.a.2.8. by 1300 when limbers will pick them up. H.Q.Dump will be at broken down tank near Bn. Hqrs. L.G.limbers will be sent to Coys. before we move.

10. Bn.H.Q. will close here at 1600 and open at new area on arrival at place to be notified later.

11. Acknowledge.

Issued at 1300.

T. Drummond Shiels
Capt. & Adjt.,
1/4th. Royal Scots(Q.R.R.)

SECRET.

APP IV War Diary

I/4th Bn. The ROYAL SCOTS (Q.E.R.).

Bn. Order No. 3I
by
Major J. Mowat Slater, D.S.O., Commanding.

Ref. Map: LENS I/I00,000. I9th October I918.

I. The Brigade will move to CHATEAU de la HAYE today, I9th inst.

2. 4th Royal Scots will pass Q.M.Stores at 0855 in the following order; Bn. H.Q., "A","B","C","D" Coys., Transport. From starting point usual intervals will be maintained.

3. Reveille 0530. Breakfast, 0700.

4. Blankets will be rolled by sections and dumped at Q.M. Stores, properly labelled, by 0600. Greatcoats will be rolled in section bundles and dumped at Q.M.Stores at 0700. "D" Coy. will provide loading party of two complete sections, to report to Quarter-Master by 0700. Officers' kits will be dumped at Q.M.Stores at 0700.

5. Lewis Gun limbers will report to Coys. at 0800, and Coys. mess baskets and stores will be sent to Bn. H.Q. mess at 0800. Maltese cart will report Aid Post at same hour.

6. Billets and their surroundings will be left scrupulously clean and certificate will be handed to the Adjutant by 0830 to this effect.

7. One motor lorry will report Q.M.Stores 0700 to clear blankets and surplus stores. This lorry may be used for a second journey if necessary. Lieut. H.J.Jones,MC.,will be in charge and lorry will rendezvous at Q.M.Stores, 7th Royal Scots at 0745. Lieut. Jones will report to A/Staff Captain at CHATEAU de la HAYE to be shown new area.
One motor lorry will be provided in the afternoon to take greatcoats to new area. O.C.,H.Q.Coy. will be responsible for detailing two N.C.Os. and 6 men of Band as guard on greatcoats and for cleaning up area, and for sending one man to Brigade H.Q. at 0900 to guide lorry for greatcoats to Q.M.Stores.

8. ACKNOWLEDGE.

(sd) T.Drummond Wilson,
Capt.& Adjt.
I/4th Bn. The ROYAL SCOTS (Q.E.R.).

Issued at 0030.

*App II

Battn Order No 29.

(1) The Bde is moving to new Bivouac area in J 2, 3 & 4 near LOUVERVAL today.

(2) Companies will move in following order: Bn H.Q. A. B. C & D

(3) The Bn will be ready to move off at 0800.

(4) Transport is moving with the Bn. L.G. Limbers & mess cart will be at H.Q. by 0730 where Coys will immediately load up.

(5) An advance party of 1 N.C.O per Coy & 1 Officer from Bn H.Q. will meet Staff Capt. at Road junction J 5 c. 9. 2. at 1000 to be pointed out new bivouac area.

(6) Usual distances will be maintained on march.

(7) Winter time came into force this morning & watches will therefore be put back an hour.

(8) Route to be followed will be Rd junction E 28 a. 2. 0 thence by CAMBRAI-BAPAUME Rd.

(9) Acknowledge.

Issued @ 0300
6-10-18.

T. Drummond [illegible]
Capt & Adjt
[illegible]

1/4 Bn The Royal Scots Bn Ord No 30

APP III

(1) Ref maps 1/20000 Sheet 57c NE + NW
1/100 000 LENS.

(1) 156 Bde will move to the XVIII
Corps area by rail and road
on 9th to TINCQUES

(2) The Battn will concentrate on
road beside Bn Hqrs at 0900 all
officers will be dismounted. March
will be to VAULX VRAUCOURT
Station. Order of march will
be Battn Hq. D C B A. (3) Coys
will render a state showing
number of personnel proceeding
by train by 0730. All details
with exception of Battn Transport
will accompany Battn and will
march with their Coys.

(4) All tents and shelters will
be returned to QM Stores by 0700
Officers kits cooking utensils and
mess baskets will be returned at

(c) Battn Entraining Officer will be 2Lt H J JONES M C and Battn Detraining Officer will be Lt A. R. CARE

(d) The minimum amount of mess stores will be dumped with officers valises at QM Stores by 0700.

8. Separate orders are being issued to the QM + T.O.

T Drummond Hulson

7/10/18

Capt & Adj
4 Bn The Royal Scots
O.G.R.

the same time to QM stores.

(5). Unconsumed portion of todays ration and rations for 8th will be carried by the men. Full water bottles will be carried and water carts will entrain full.

(6) Areas occupied by Coys & Bn Hq must be left scrupulously clean.

(7) (a) At the detraining point OC B Coy will detail an unloading party of his two strongest platoons under an officer as an unloading party for the Bde. This party will report on arrival to the detraining officer Lt J Austin and will remain on duty at the station until the arrival of the last train.

(b) OC C Coy will detail one platoon to unload the Rations Baggage

1/4th. Bn. The Royal Scots (Q.E.R.) APP. V

BATTALION ORDER No. 34
by
Major J. Mowat Slater, D.S.O., Comdg.

- -

Ref. Map Sheets 44 & 44a, 1/40,000. 23rd. October, 1918.

1. The 52nd. Division is concentrating in FLINES area tomorrow, 24th. Oct. 1918.

2. The 156th. Bde. will move by march route to COUTICHES and MOLINEL in the following order:-
7th. Royal Scots, Bde. H.Q., 7th. Sco. Rifles,
156th. L.T.M.Bty., 4th. Royal Scots.
The Bn. will move off in the following order:-
H.Q., "D", "C", "B", "A" Coys.,
and will be drawn up ready to move off at 0950. There will be no halt for midday meal.

3. Transport and baggage wagons will march with units.

4. Parade hours for tomorrow:- Reveille 0600, Sick Parade 0630, Bresjfast 0715.
Dress:- Marching order less blankets and greatcoats. These will be dumped at Q.M.Stores at 0700 rolled in section bundles. They will be brought forward in motor lorries. Officers kits will be dumped at Q.M. Stores at 0800.

5. Advance party of Lieut. McEwan and 1 O.R. from Bn.H.Q. will report to the A/Staff Captain at 1000 on the road junction at M.2.d.4.5. and will be allotted billets. They will meet the Bn. on the road junction at M.8.a.8.4. and guide them to their billets.

6. Motor lorries. One motor lorry will be brought from Bde.H.Q. at 0700, a guide being sent from Bn.H.Q. to guide it to Bn.H.Q. This motor lorry will not do more than two trips unless absolutely necessary.

7. Supplies. Rations drawn for consumption on the 25th. inst. will be delivered by supply wagons on arrival at COUTICHES area. After delivery of rations supply wagons will return to H.Q., 219th.Coy. COUTICHES, R.P. at same place.

8. Divisional Reception Camp is moving tomorrow to VITRY EN ARTOIS. Men going onleave for sailing date 27th. inst. will report there.

9. Billets will be left clean.

10. Bn. H.Q. will close at present location at 0930 and will open at COUTICHES on arrival there.

11. ACKNOWLEDGE.

Copies to:-
"A" Coy.
"B" "
"C" "
"D" "
H.Q. Coy.
H.Q. Mess.
T.O.
Q.M.
OFFICE
WAR DIARY.

T. Drummond Wilson
Capt. & Adjt.,
1/4th. Royal Scots (Q.E.R.)

+=+=+=+=+=+=+=+=+=+=+=+=+=+=+=+

SECRET.

Copy No. 11

APP(6)

1/4th. Bn. The Royal Scots (Q.E.R.)

BATTALION ORDER No. 37
by
Major J. Mowat Slater, D.S.O., Comdg.

- -

Ref. Map Sheet 44, 1/40,000. 28th. October, 1918.

1. The 52nd. Division is relieving the 12th. Division on 28th. Oct. and night 28th/29th. Oct. 1918. The 156th. Inf. Bde. is relieving the 36th. Inf. Bde. in the front line of the Divl. Sector.

2. The 4th. Royal Scots will relieve the 9th. Royal Fusiliers in Left Support. This relief will take place this afternoon and Companies ought to be ready to move any time after 1330. Dress, full marching order - men will wear their steel helmets.

3. Details of the relief will be intimated to O.C. Coys. later.

4. Companies will forward to Bn. H.Q. by 0900 tomorrow, 29th. inst., a statement or sketch shewing their dispositions.

5. Medical. Car Post at J.34.a.6.5. A.D.S. at I.36.a.6.7. Bn. Aid Post will be notified later.

6. Rations will be delivered daily to transport lines by 219th. Coy. A.S.C. Q.M. Stores will be located at Transport Lines.

7. All 1/20,000 maps sheets 44NE and 44SE should be taken over. A report will be rendered to Bn.H.Q. as to numbers taken over.

8. Completion of relief will be wired to Bn.H.Q. by code word "P.C.99".

9. The location of Bn.H.Q. will be notified later.

10. Acknowledge.

Issued at 0945.

T. Drummond Shiels
Capt. & Adjt.,
1/4th. Royal Scots (Q.E.R.)

Copy No. 1 Office.
2 "A" Coy.
3 "B" "
4 "C" "
5 "D" "
6 H.Q. Mess
7 H.Q. Coy.
8 T.O.
9 Q.M.
10 M.O.
11 War Diary
12 War Diary.

Confidential

1/4th Bn The Royal Scots (Q & 10)

WAR DIARY

for

NOVEMBER

1918

Vol XLII

VR 8

Instructions regarding War Diaries and Intelligence Summaries are contained in F. S. Regs., Part II. and the Staff Manual respectively. Title pages will be prepared in manuscript.

WAR DIARY
or
INTELLIGENCE SUMMARY.
(Erase heading not required.)

Army Form C. 2118.

(P1.)

1/4th Bn The Royal Scots — November 1918.

Volume XLII

Place	Date	Hour	Summary of Events and Information	Remarks and references to Appendices
FRESNOY. Ref Map 1/20000 FRANCE SHEET 44 NE	1st Nov 1918		The Bn remained at its present quarters until the night of the 4/5th when it took over posts held by the 7th Scottish Rifles on the EAST side of the SCARPE RIVER from CHATEAU de MONTAGNE to CHATEAU L'ABBE.	[illegible]
Ref Map FRANCE 1/20000 Sheet 45 NW	9th		The enemy having retreated orders were issued to pursue him & the Bn crossed the R. ESCAUT RIVER & JARD CANAL & pushed on to BLATON where it billetted for the night.	[illegible]
	10		The Bn moved off from BLATON at 0715 as advance guard for the 156th Inf Bde see (app. 1) & pushed forward to SIRAULT where it took up a position covering the Divisional front. During its progress through the various villages it was received with the greatest enthusiasm by the inhabitants who were more than delighted to be liberated from the oppression of the Hun.	App. 1
HERCHIES.			At 1500 the Bde again moved off the 7th Sco Rifles taking up the outpost line & marched to HERCHIES where the Bn billetted. During the march the enemy shelled the roads & also machine gunned them but casualties only amounted to three O Ranks wounded.	[illegible]
	11		There was great jubilation when the news came through that	

A6945 Wt. W11422/M1160 350,000 12/16 D. D. & L. Forms/C./2118/14.

Army Form C. 2118.

Instructions regarding War Diaries and Intelligence Summaries are contained in F. S. Regs., Part II, and the Staff Manual respectively. Title pages will be prepared in manuscript.

WAR DIARY
or
INTELLIGENCE SUMMARY.
(Erase heading not required.)

1/4th Bn The Royal Scots — November 1918 — (P. 2.) Page (2)

Place	Date	Hour	Summary of Events and Information	Remarks and references to Appendices
			Volume XLII	
	11		the enemy had accepted defeat & that hostilities ceased at 1100.	TSW
	12th – 14th		Interior Economy gone into & men smartened up generally	TSW.
	15th		This Battalion supplied 80 Other Ranks for a parade of the Army Commanders Official entry into MONS. Major Slater DSO was in command of the 156th Inf Brigade party. The party lined the streets at the Official entry & then marched past the Army Commander in the GRAND PLACE	TSW
	16		Inspection of Battalion Transport by the B G C	TSW
	17		Thanksgiving services were held today. In the morning there was a Divisional service at which each Battalion sent one Company & the Commanding Officer & Adjutant attended. In the afternoon a Brigade service was held when the whole Brigade turned out. The service was of a simple but impressive nature. The cold was intense & men wore their leather jerkins for first time on parade.	TSW

A6945 Wt. W11422/M1160 350,000 12/16 D. D. & L. Forms/C./2118/14.

Instructions regarding War Diaries and Intelligence Summaries are contained in F. S. Regs., Part II. and the Staff Manual respectively. Title pages will be prepared in manuscript.

WAR DIARY
or
INTELLIGENCE SUMMARY.
(Erase heading not required.)

Army Form C. 2118.

(P. 3.)

1/4th Bn The Royal Scots — November 1918

Place	Date	Hour	Summary of Events and Information	Remarks and references to Appendices
			Volume XLII	
HERCHIES	18th – 28th		Ordinary routine was carried out, three hours military training including ceremonial.	TSU
MONTIGNIES LEZ LENS.	28th – 30		Battalion moved to new billeting area at this village & prepared to make its winter quarters here	TSU
			General Information	
			The month has been an eventful one & one likely never to be forgotten by all who took part in the Battalions progress to HERCHIES.	
			The health of the Battalion has been exceedingly good. The usual strength return is attached. (app 2)	TSU

T. Drummond [illegible]
Capt & Adjutant
1/4th Bn The Royal Scots

A6945 Wt. W11422/M1160 350,000 12/16 D. D. & L. Forms/C./2118/14.

(APP. 7)

1/4th Bn The Royal Scots Bn Order No 41 Copy

Ref Map: 1/20000 Sheet 45 N.W. 10-XI-18.

(1) As far as is known there is no enemy W. of MONS except possibly a few snipers in BOIS de BAUDOUR.

(2) Canadian Corps has taken VILLE POMMEREUL and are working N + E.

(3) 157th Inf Bde are approximately in line with us on our Right but 175 Inf Bde are more than 5 miles behind on our left.

(4) 52nd Division continue the advance Eastwards today

(a) 156th Inf Bde will advance Eastwards today covered by an advance under command of Major T. MOWAT SLATER D.S.O.

(b) Advance Guard will consist of
4th The Royal Scots
"B" Coy. 52 M.G. Bn.
+ 2 Platoons VIII Corps Cyclists

(c) B Coy M.G. Bn. will report H.Q. 4th Royal Scots at 0715 + the 2 platoons of VIII Corps Cyclists at 0700.

(d) The leading troops of the Advance Guard will leave the line G.23.a.9.6 to G.17.A.0.6 at 0800.

Northern + Southern Bde Boundaries

are : Northern :- E. + W. line through G. 6. central. Southern. E. + W. line through G. 24. Central

(5) Composition of advance Guard:-

Vanguard will consist of D Coy.

Main guard C. B. A. Coys. B. Coy. 5? ...

Separate orders are being given to the 2 platoons of Cyclists attached to the Advance Guard.

Vanguard will leave cross roads at G. 17. D. 9. 7. at 0800 + move along the road to G. 18. Central to H. 13. A. + B - H. 14. A + B. - + H. 15. A - H. 9. C. + D + running Eastwards to H. 11. D - H. 12. C + D. to SIRAULT.

B. A + HQ Coys. will pass starting point at G. 15. a. 9. 1. at 0715 + join C Coy at G. 17. D. 9. 7.

(6) The following objectives will be made good by the Advance Guard:-

(a) The Road between PONT de CALVAIRE + H. 20. B. 2. 0.

(b) The line of the road H. 4. central - H. 11. A. 2. 3. - H. 17. D. 2. 6 - H. 23. C. 8. 7.

(3)

(c) The Railway line running through I.1.B.D – I.7.B.D – I.13.B – I.20.A.
Reports will be forwarded by Vanguard + attached cyclists to Head of main guard when these objectives are reached.

7. L.G. limbers, magazine limbers, medical cart + 1 Tool cart will march in rear of advance Guard. The remainder of 1st + 2nd line Transport will march brigaded under B.T.O.
Administrative Portion + Transport will await orders from B.T.O. at Bn HQ at 0830.
C + D Coys will send cookers back to Bn HQ by 0800.

8. 4 Royal Scots will not proceed beyond last objective.

9. Acknowledge.

T. Drummond Shiels
Capt + Adj
4th Bn The Royal Scots (QR)

Appendix 2

War Diary November 1918 — APP II — Strengths of Batt^n at 30/11/18

Additions to Strength

	Off	OR
Reinforcements	6	91
" at Div^l Rec^n Camp	-	31
From Hospital	2	84
Cross posted from 7th R Scots	3	
	11	206

Deductions from Strength

	Off	OR
Transf^d to U.K	4	-
OR^s now in Hosp^l over 7 days	-	28
Casualties - Wounded	-	4
Batman at Corps Hdqrs now struck off	-	1
To Hospital (sick)	-	29
	4	62

Strengths of Batt^n at 30/11/18

	Off	OR
With Battalion	30	639
Batt^n Transport	1	53
att^d Bde & T.M. Batty "	-	2
Courses of Instruction	2	6
On Leave to UK	2	53
Detached	1	29
Guards etc	-	12
att^d 9th Bde R.F.A	1	1
Reinforcements advised from Div^l Rec^n Camp	-	31
In Hospital (ORs under 7 days)	6	13
Total	43	839

Attached to Batt^n

	Off	OR
Medical Officer	1	-
P.T Instructor	-	1
Belgian Interpreter	-	1
	1	2

T. Drummond Wilson
Capt & Adjutant
1/4 Bn The Royal Scots

Instructions regarding War Diaries and Intelligence Summaries are contained in F. S. Regs., Part II. and the Staff Manual respectively. Title pages will be prepared in manuscript.

WAR DIARY
or
INTELLIGENCE SUMMARY.
(Erase heading not required.)

Army Form C. 2118.

Original

Place	Date	Hour	Summary of Events and Information	Remarks and references to Appendices
			Confidential	
			War Diary	
			of	
			156th Trench Mortar Battery	
			1st to 30th November 1918	
			Volume XVI	

A6945 Wt. W11422/M1160 350,000 12/16 D. D. & L. Forms/C./2118/14.

156th M.G. Battery

Instructions regarding War Diaries and Intelligence Summaries are contained in F. S. Regs., Part II. and the Staff Manual respectively. Title pages will be prepared in manuscript.

Sheet No 1

WAR DIARY
or
INTELLIGENCE SUMMARY.
(Erase heading not required.)

Army Form C. 2118.

Place	Date	Hour	Summary of Events and Information	Remarks and references to Appendices
Battery H.Q. MONT PROY	1/11/18		Two guns in the line in BRUILLE No 2 Section.	
			2 ORs reported for duty from leave in UK.	N.J.D.
	2/11/18		Rifle & equipment inspections 2 ORs admitted to Field Ambulance (Sick)	N.J.D.
	3/11/18		Rifle Inspection 1 OR struck off effective strength as from 3/11/18.	
			No 2 Section relieved by No 1 Section. Fired 19 rounds at enemy M.G.s at	N.J.D.
			K 26 A 8.9	
	4/11/18		Fired 18 rounds at M.G.s in K 26 A 8.9. 1 OR proceeded on 14 days	N.J.D.
			leave to UK.	
	5/11/18		Cleaning guns & ammunition	N.J.D.
	6/11/18		do 1 OR reported for duty from leave in UK	N.J.D.
	7/11/18		Fired 19 rounds at M.G.s in K 26 A 8.9. 2 ORs do	N.J.D.
	8/11/18		Battery moved from MONT PROY to HERNIES stayed overnight	N.J.D.
	9/11/18		Marched to BLATON & stayed overnight.	N.J.D.
	10/11/18		Marched to HERCHIES	N.J.D.
HERCHIES	11/11/18		Hostilities ceased at 1100 & battery moved into billets	N.J.D.
	12/11/18		Resting	N.J.D.

A6945 Wt. W11422/M1160 350,000 12/16 D. D. & L. Forms/C./2118/14.

136th T.M. Battery

Instructions regarding War Diaries and Intelligence Summaries are contained in F. S. Regs., Par. II. and the Staff Manual respectively. Title pages will be prepared in manuscript.

Sheet No 8

WAR DIARY
or
INTELLIGENCE SUMMARY.
(Erase heading not required.)

Army Form C. 2118.

Place	Date	Hour	Summary of Events and Information	Remarks and references to Appendices
HERCHIES	13/11/18		Rifle & Kit inspections. Capt Jas Scott resumed command of the Battery as from todays date	NJD
	14/11/18		Training during forenoon. Lt Trotter proceeded on 14 days leave to UK. 1 OR admitted to hospital (PUO)	NJD
	15/11/18		Training during forenoon. 2 ORs reported for duty from GHQ course	NJD
	16/11/18		Training during forenoon. 4 ORs proceeded on 14 days leave to UK. 1 OR reported for duty from leave in UK.	NJD
			Battery Transport inspected by BGC	
	17/11/18		Divine Service	NJD
	18/11/18		Training as usual	NJD
	19/11/18		Battery inspected by BGC	NJD
	20/11/18		Training as usual 1 OR reported for duty from leave in UK.	NJD
	21/11/18		do 1 OR proceeded on 14 days leave to UK	NJD
	22/11/18		do 1 OR struck struck off effective strength as from 22/11/18	NJD

A6945 Wt. W11422/M1160 350,000 12/16 D. D. & L. Forms/C./2118/14.

13th T.M. Battery

Instructions regarding War Diaries and Intelligence Summaries are contained in F. S. Regs., Par. II. and the Staff Manual respectively. Title pages will be prepared in manuscript.

Sheet No. 3.

WAR DIARY
or
INTELLIGENCE SUMMARY.
(Erase heading not required.)

Army Form C. 2118.

Place	Date	Hour	Summary of Events and Information	Remarks and references to Appendices
HERCHIES	23/11/18		Training as usual 1 OR reported for duty from leave in UK	NJD
	24/11/18		Divine Service.	NJD
	25/11/18		Training as usual	NJD
	26/11/18		do 2/Lt W.A. Hillard proceeded on 14 days leave to UK	NJD
	27/11/18		Training as usual	NJD
	28/11/18		Battery moved to MONTIGNIES LES. LENS.	NJD
	29/11/18		Rifle & billet inspections cleaning equipment etc	NJD
	30/11/18		St Andrews' Day "Holiday"	
			Battery moved to THORICOURT.	NJD
			1 OR proceeded on 14 days leave to UK	

A6945 Wt. W11422/M1160 350,000 12/16 D. D. & L. Forms/C./2118/14.

156th T M Battery

Instructions regarding War Diaries and Intelligence Summaries are contained in F. S. Regs., Part II. and the Staff Manual respectively. Title pages will be prepared in manuscript.

Sheet No 4

WAR DIARY
or
INTELLIGENCE SUMMARY.
(Erase heading not required.)

Army Form C. 2118.

Place	Date	Hour	Summary of Events and Information	Remarks and references to Appendices
THORICOURT	30/11/18		Personnel of Battery at this date	
			Officers Other ranks	
			2 1/4th Royal Scots 17. 1/4th Royal Scots	NS
			2 1/7th Royal Scots 15. 1/7th Royal Scots	
			4 8. 1/7th Scottish Rifles	
			7. 1/8th Scottish Rifles	
			47.	
			J. McSmith Capt	
			Commdg 156th T M Battery	

A6945 Wt. W11422/M1160 350,000 12/16 D. D. & L. Forms/C./2118/14.

Confidential

Original

VR 9

War Diary

of

1/4th/13th The Royal Scots (Q.R.)

from

1st to 31st DECEMBER 1918

(Vol XLIII)

Instructions regarding War Diaries and Intelligence Summaries are contained in F. S. Regs., Part II. and the Staff Manual respectively. Title pages will be prepared in manuscript.

WAR DIARY
or
INTELLIGENCE SUMMARY.
(Erase heading not required.)

Army Form C. 2118.

P. 1

1/4 Bn. The Royal Scots — December 1918.

Place	Date	Hour	Summary of Events and Information	Remarks and references to Appendices
			Volume XLIII	
	DEC. 1918			
MONTIGNIES-LES-LENS			During December the Bn. settled down to a regular routine of Training, – Military, Educational and Recreational. Lieut-Colonel A. Maclaine Mitchell, D.S.O. re-assumed command on 8th Dec. On 13th Decr. the Bn. was inspected by the G.O.C. 52nd (Lowland) Division.	G.J.
			Educational schemes were further developed, and progress has been well maintained, suitable men being despatched to various short Courses as vacancies occurred. A large number of men continue to apply themselves diligently and earnestly to their Educational work.	
			Special attention has been given to Recreational Training, and the arrangements made for Football, Boxing, Dancing and Games have been taken advantage of with enthusiasm. Preparations were made for a Bn. Sports Meeting to be held on 1st Jan. A Battalion Concert Party has been formed and has met with such success as to warrant further encouragement of the project. Special arrangements were made for Christmas festivities, while the matter of voting in the General Election received attention.	G.J.

A6945 Wt. W11422/M1160 350,000 12/16 D. D. & L. Forms/C./2118/14.

Army Form C. 2118.

Instructions regarding War Diaries and Intelligence Summaries are contained in F. S. Regs., Part II. and the Staff Manual respectively. Title pages will be prepared in manuscript.

WAR DIARY
or
INTELLIGENCE SUMMARY.

(Erase heading not required.)

1/4th Bn. The Royal Scots (QRR) December 1918 - P 2

Place	Date	Hour	Summary of Events and Information	Remarks and references to Appendices
			Volume XLIII	
	DEC 1918.		The Military Medal was awarded to 201048 Pte. A. Wiseman on 23rd Dec (156 Bde. SC. 408)	
			The following officers joined Bn. during the month:-	
			2/Lieut. H. Jones, 3rd Dec. 2/Lieut A. O. Rankine 3rd Dec.	G.G.
			2/Lieut J. J. S. Morton-Robertson, 6th Dec. 2/Lieut. R. S. Aitchison. 6th Dec.	
			The health of the Battalion continues excellent	
			The usual strength return is attached. (see App I)	G.G.
			George Gibson Capt a/Adjt 1/4th Bn The Royal Scots	

A6945 Wt. W11422/M1160 350,000 12/16 D. D. & L. Forms/C./2118/14.

Appendix I

Attachment to War Diary of 1/4 Bn The Royal Scots (Q.R.) December 1918

Additions to Strength

	Off	O.R.
From Hospl.	1	54
Reinforcements	3	1
	4	55

Deductions from Strength

	Off	O.R.
Now in Hospl over 7 days	-	13
Transferred to U.K. (sick)	3	-
" " Home estabt.	-	3
" " Labour Corps	1	2
Admitted to Hospital	-	28
A.S.C. Officer struck off on proceeding to M.T. Course	1	
	5	46

Strength of Battalion 31/12/18

	Off	O.R.
With Battalion (cys) & Bn. Hdqrs	28 5	597 106
Transport	1	64
Bde & Bde T.M. Bty Transport	-	2
Detached	2	33
On Leave to U.K.	3	18
Absent without leave	-	1
Brigade Guard & Runners	-	12
On duty at 1/2 L.F.A. as Interpreter	-	1
In Hospital (under 7 days)	1	5
Courses of Instruction	2	9
Total	42	848

Attached to Battalion

	Off	O.R.
R.A.M.C. (Medical Officer)	1	-
R.C. Chaplain	1	-
Billet Warden	-	1
from Divl. RE Signals	-	2
" 412 & 413 Fld Coy R.E.	-	7
Belgium Interpreter	-	1
" Gendarme	-	1
Total	2	12

George Gibson
Lt Col Cdg
1/4 Bn the Royal Scots

Confidential

98

War Diary

of

1/4th Battn The Royal Scots (Q.R.)

for

January 1919.

Vol. XLIV

1/4 R Scots

98 10

52

Instructions regarding War Diaries and Intelligence Summaries are contained in F. S. Regs., Part II, and the Staff Manual respectively. Title pages will be prepared in manuscript.

WAR DIARY or INTELLIGENCE SUMMARY.

(Erase heading not required.)

P. 1.

Army Form C. 2118.

1/4th Bn. The Royal Scots — January 1919

Place	Date	Hour	VOLUME XLIV — Summary of Events and Information	Remarks and references to Appendices
Montignies-lez-Lens	Jan 1919		The Battalion inaugurated the New Year with a successful Sports meeting on 1st January, and with suitable functions of a festive nature; thereafter the usual military training was proceeded with.	
	Jan. 8th		On 8th January 1919, the General Officer Commanding 52nd (Lowland) Division presented Military Medals and M.S. Ribbons at a ceremonial parade at Montignies-lez-Lens, the Battalion ~~by~~ being represented by eight recipients of Military Medals.	TBW
	JAN. 18th		On 18th January the Battalion took part in a ceremonial parade at MAISIERES at which the Corps Commander presented ribbons to Other Ranks belonging to the Division, who had been awarded the Military Cross or Distinguished Conduct Medal but who had not had their ribbons presented. Three men of the Battalion, who had been awarded Distinguished Conduct Medals, were presented with the ribbons on this occasion.	TBW
			During the month Educational Training continued and progressed, while Recreational Training becomes ever a more important item of	TBW

A6945 Wt. W11422/M1160 350,000 12/16 D. D. & L. Forms/C./2118/14.

Army Form C. 2118.

Instructions regarding War Diaries and Intelligence Summaries are contained in F. S. Regs., Part II. and the Staff Manual respectively. Title pages will be prepared in manuscript.

WAR DIARY
or
INTELLIGENCE SUMMARY.

(*Erase heading not required.*)

P. 2.

1/4th Bn. The Royal Scots — January 1919

Vol. XLIV

Place	Date	Hour	Summary of Events and Information	Remarks and references to Appendices
	Jan.	1919	the daily programme. Every advantage has been taken of the facilities available for recreation for the men of the Battalion, including visits to the Waterloo Battlefield, Concerts, the opening of recreation rooms and libraries, and the usual sports and games. Demobilization, on the lines laid down by Higher Authority, has proceeded steadily, 5 Officers and 160 Other Ranks proceeding en Route to U.K. during the month.	
			The health of the Battalion has been excellent.	
			The usual strength return is attached.	
			T. Drummond Watson Capt. & Adjt. 1/4 Bn. The Royal Scots (Q.E.R.)	

A6945 Wt. W11422/M1160 350,000 12/16 D. D. & L. Forms/C./2118/14.

Attachment to War Diary January 1919

Additions to Strength

	Off	OR
Reinforcements	-	8
From Hospital	-	30
	-	38

Deductions from Strength

	Off	OR
Now in Hospl over 7 days	-	5
Reposted to 2nd R Scots	-	2
Embarked for U.K for Demobilisation	1	24
Transf^d to R.G.A.	-	1
" " R.F.A	-	1
Admitted to Hospital	-	16
	1	49

Strength at 30th January 1919

	Off	OR
With Battalion	29	574
Battalion Transport	1	55
att^d Bde Transport		1
On Leave to U.K.	3	15
Courses of Instruction	1	6
Runners att^d Bde Hdqrs	-	3
Detached	2	43
Absent while on leave to UK	-	1
On duty as Interpreter at 1/2 L.F.A	-	1
Proceeded to UK for Demobilisation, & still included in effective Str. Pending notifn of Embn from D.A.G.	4	136
In Hospital (over under) 7 days	1	2
	41	834

Personnel attached to Battalion:-

	Off	OR
Medical Officer	1	-
R.C. Chaplain	1	-
Belgian Interpreter	-	1
Billet Warden	-	1
P.T & B.F Instructor	-	1
	2	3

T Drummond [illegible]
Capt & Adjt
4th Bn The Royal Scots

Confidential

9811

War Diary

of

1/4th Bn. The Royal Scots

for

February 1919.

- Vol XLV. -

8A

Army Form C. 2118.

Instructions regarding War Diaries and Intelligence Summaries are contained in F. S. Regs., Part II. and the Staff Manual respectively. Title pages will be prepared in manuscript.

WAR DIARY
or
INTELLIGENCE SUMMARY.
(*Erase heading not required.*)

1/4th Bn The Royal Scots

Place	Date	Hour	Summary of Events and Information	Remarks and references to Appendices
			Volume XLV February 1919	
Montignies les Lens Belgium			Demobilisation has proceeded steadily during the month. A Draft of all retainable men is under orders to proceed to join the Army of Occupation; when this draft proceeds, the Battalion will be at cadre strength. The men have been kept fit by healthy games, lectures & the Bn concert party has largely contributed to the cheerfulness of all ranks. The health of the Battalion has been splendid. The usual strength return is appended.	
			T. Drummond Tulse Capt & Adjutant 1/4th Bn The Royal Scots.	

A6945 Wt. W11422/M1160 350,000 12/16 D. D. & L. Forms/C./2118/14.

Appendix to War Diary February 1919. 1/4th Bn The Royal Scots (Q.R.)

Additions to Strength

	Off	OR
From Hospital	-	6
	-	6

Deductions from Strength

	Off	OR
Demobilised while on Leave to U.K.	-	9
Embarked for Demobn (in Hospl)	7	196
Died while proceeding for Demobn	-	1
To Pool of Clerks at Base	-	2
" duty at XXII Corps Concentration Camps	1	2
Evacuated to U.K.	1	-
To Hospital	-	4
	9	214

Strength of Battalion as at 28/2/19.

	Off.	OR
With Battalion		
Coys & Bn Hdqrs	15	212
Transport	1	27
On Leave to U.K.	1	8
Detached	8	19
Absent without Leave	-	1
Guarding Supplies Trains at Bethune	-	23
Proceeded to U.K. for Demobilisation (still on effective strength pending notifn of embarkn)	6	334
In Hospital (ORs under 7 days)	1	5
	32	629

Personnel attached to Unit (not included above)

	Off	OR
Medical Officer	1	-
R.C. Chaplain	1	-
Belgian Interpreter	-	1
Prisoner from 156 Bde T.M. Batty	-	1
	2	2

Confidential

War Diary

of

1/4th Bn The Royal Scots (Q.R.)

for

MARCH 1919

Vol. XLVI

Vol 12

Instructions regarding War Diaries and Intelligence Summaries are contained in F. S. Regs., Part II. and the Staff Manual respectively. Title pages will be prepared in manuscript.

Army Form C. 2118.

WAR DIARY
or
~~INTELLIGENCE SUMMARY.~~
(Erase heading not required.)

Volume XLVI

MARCH 1919

Place	Date	Hour	Summary of Events and Information	Remarks and references to Appendices
Montignies-les-Lens, BELGIUM.	1st. to 17th.		Demobilization of the Battalion was completed during the month.	
			Lieut.Colonel A.MACLAINE MITCHELL D.S.O., assumed command of 156th Inf.Bde. on 5th March on Brig.General A.H. LEGGETT C.M.G. D.S.O., proceeding to U.K.	
			The Draft of Volunteer and Retainable Officers and Other Ranks, mentioned in War Diary of February, proceeded to join 11th Bn. The Royal Scots on the Rhine on 11th March, under command of Lieut.A/Capt. H.W. WINCHESTER,M.C. - Strength of Draft, 9 Officers 186 Other Ranks. The other Officers of the Draft were:-	
			Lieut. J. ALEXANDER. — 2/Lieut. S.J. CORNFORD.	
			" G.S. YOUNG, M.C. (attached from 15th Bn.) — 2/Lieut. H. JONES.	
			" W.W. KELLY. — 2/LIEUT. C. BRUCE. (attached from 3rd. Bn.)	
			" J.S. MARSLAND. — 2/Lieut. D.R. BREMNER.	
			Lieut.A/Capt. R.McEWAN also volunteered for the Army of Occupation, but was absent on leave in U.K. when the Draft left. On his return he will join 11th Bn. 27 Other Ranks, on duty away from the Battalion at the time the Draft proceeded, will also go forward later.	TBW.
Soignies, BELGIUM.	17th to 31st.		On departure of this Draft, the Battalion was reduced to cadre strength, and, on the 17th of the Month, proceeded under command of Major J. MOWAT SLATER,D.S.O., to SOIGNIES (rendezvous of /	

D. D. & L., London, E.C. (A7883) Wt. W809/M1672 350,000 4/17 Sch. 52a Forms/C/2118/14

Army Form C. 2118.

WAR DIARY
or
~~INTELLIGENCE SUMMARY.~~
(Erase heading not required.)

Instructions regarding War Diaries and Intelligence Summaries are contained in F. S. Regs., Part II. and the Staff Manual respectively. Title pages will be prepared in manuscript.

Volume XLVI — MARCH 1919.

Place	Date	Hour	Summary of Events and Information	Remarks and references to Appendices
Soignies, BELGIUM.	17th to 31st.		/of the Division), there to await orders for Home.	
			The following Officers were demobilized :-	
			16th March - Lieut. A/Capt. G.W. EAKINS, M.C. 27th. March- Lieut. J. Gardine	
			19th March - 2/Lieut. T.C.LAWSON. 27th. March- 2/ Lieut. W. F.Johnston	
			23rd March - 2/ " D.K.M. CORDON. 27th. March- 2/ Lieut. A. MacDougal	
			" " - 2/ " C.P. WRIGHT.	
			" " - 2/ " A. MACKENZIE.	
			The health of the Battalion during the Month was excellent.	
			Statement showing Strength and casualties is attached.	
			Lieut. (A/Capt.) R. McEwan and the 14 Other Ranks Pproceeded to join the 11th. Bn. The Royal Scots on the 29th. inst.	

T. Drummond Wilson
CAPT. & ADJT.
1/4th. Bn. The Royal Scots (Q.E.R.)

D. D. & L., London, E.C. (A7883) Wt. W809/M1672 350,000 4/17 Sch. 52a Forms/C/2118/14

Attachment to WAR DIARY for March 1919. I/4th Bn. The Royal Scots (Q.E.R.)

Additions to Strength

	Off.	O.R.s
- NIL -	"	"

Deductions from Strength

	Off.	O.Rs.
Now in Hospital over 7days	"	2
To hospital during the Month	"	2
Embarked to U.K. for Demobilisation	7	340
Transferred to R.E.	-	1
Proceeded to U.K. having re-enlisted	-	11
Now taken on the Cadre Estab. of 156 Bde Hdqrs	-	3
Absent without Leave and now struck off on court of Enquiry being held	-	1
Posted & proceeded to join 11th Bn. The Royal Scots on 11/3/19	10	186
Do " 30/3/19	-	14
Posted to 11th Royal Scots (from Bde Employ, " Div. ", " Extra Reg. Employ etc)	-	12
	17	571

Strength of Battalion as at 31st March 1919.

	Off.	OR
With Unit:-		
Cadre x	4	47
Releasable	1	2
On Detached duty	1	2
To Base I/c of Animals x (Cadre)	-	1
Proceeded to U.K. (for Demobilisation, but still on Effective Strength pending notn. of Embarkn.)	8	6
Sick in Hospital	1	-
	15	58

T. Drummond Shiels

CAPT. & ADJT.
1/4th. Bn. The Royal Scots (Q.E.R.)

VB 13

1/4th Bn The Royal Scots.

War Diary.

Volume XLVI April 1919.

423

1/4th Bn The Royal Scots (Q.E.R.)

Instructions regarding War Diaries and Intelligence Summaries are contained in F. S. Regs., Part II, and the Staff Manual respectively. Title pages will be prepared in manuscript.

WAR DIARY
or
~~INTELLIGENCE SUMMARY.~~
(Erase heading not required.)

Army Form C. 2118.

Place	Date	Hour	Summary of Events and Information — April 1919 — Volume XLVI	Remarks and references to Appendices
Soignies	1st – 27th		There is nothing further to report since last month. One or two men who returned from leave & hospital were demobilised. On the 27th the Cadre left Soignies at 1830 for DUNKIRK.	TDW
DUNKIRK	28th		Arrived at Dunkirk at 1430 & marched to Reception Camp, where men were taken off ~~the~~ bathed & given clean clothing, thence proceeding to Embarkation Camp. The journey down was fairly comfortable, an excellent breakfast being provided at Mons for all ranks.	TDW.
	30th		Usual strength return is attached.	TDW.

D. D. & L., London, E.C.
(A7883) Wt. W809/M1672 350,000 4/17 Sch. 52a Forms/C/2118/14

Attachment to War Diary for April 1919. 1/4th Bn. The Royal Scots (QRR)

Additions to Strength

	Off.	OR
Rejoined Bn. from Prison	-	1
" " " Hospital	-	1
	-	2

Deductions from Strength

	Off	OR
Embarked to UK for Demobn.	9	11
Ifd. to UK (while proceeding for Demobn.)	-	1
Posted to 11th Bn. Royal Scots	-	3
	9	15

Strength of Battalion as at

	Off.	OR
With Unit - Cadre Battn.	3	45
L.G. Officer on Bde duty at Soignies (to rejoin Bn. shortly)	1	-
Sick in Hospital	1	-
Draft Conducting Officer	1	-
	6	45

www.ingramcontent.com/pod-product-compliance
Lightning Source LLC
Chambersburg PA
CBHW081427160426
43193CB00013B/2208
9781474529174